The Life of a Real Certified Master Chef: The Biography of Hartmut Handke, CMC

by Hartmut Handke, CMC

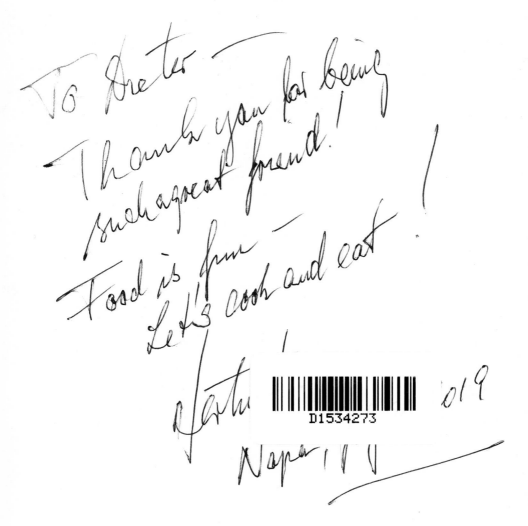

To Dieter —
Thanks you for being such a great friend!

Food is fun —
Let's cook and eat!

Harti
Napa

D1534273

019

ISBN: 9781549780806

With love to Margot - my faithful friend, ardent advisor, staunch supporter and wonderful wife.

"There is always room for improvement." ~ Ferdinand Metz

Foreword

To be clear upfront, Hartmut is a friend, valued colleague and respected culinarian, all of which may have influenced this foreword.

Master Chef Handke's extensive international experience offers a refreshing view of a chef's life and related adventures, which departs from the usual and often limited working background of many culinary authors. He truly lived and experienced the entire spectrum of foodservice from hotels to restaurants and clubs, to high-end resorts, including catering and ownership of two restaurants.

The chef's somewhat nomadic lifestyle through his early career weaves a fascinating tale, enriched by the culture, the people and the food traditions of the many countries he and his wife Margot experienced. Equally interesting is the fact that he not just visited, but actually worked in, taught, learned from and contributed to the culinary scene of many countries.

I can personally attest to Chef Handke's incredible energies, his tenacity and his outstanding culinary talent, which he brought to the US Culinary Olympic Team with whom he shared the excitement and pride of having won a World Championship.

For the aspiring culinary student, this book is a must, as it provides a sobering and realistic departure from the often perpetuated notion that the life of a professional chef is nothing but glamorous as portrayed by various media outlets. For Chef Handke's colleagues in the field, the review of his career will evoke a sense of déjà vu and a consenting smile, while for the food enthusiast or casual reader this enlightening tale of the chef's career provides an interesting look into his personal and professional life.

For me, reading his book feels like a talk with a friend in front of the fireplace over a nice glass of German Riesling, so light up the fire, relax and enjoy reading about Chef Handke's adventures.

~ Ferdinand Metz, Certified Master Chef and World Global Master Chef

Acknowledgements

I would like to thank and recognize all of the people who educated, supported, helped, worked and stayed by my side, starting with my parents, who allowed me to freely choose my profession without any interference. Unfortunately they couldn't share my success, which didn't come until they had both passed away - my mother at age 63 and my father at 73. I have a deep gratitude to Margot's parents because when I had the crazy idea of immigrating to Canada in 1962, they agreed to let Margot come along not knowing whether they would see her again. That must have been a very difficult decision for them. I'm very thankful for Margot, my partner of more than 50 years, who stuck with me every day of our life together. I would not be the person I am today without her. A big thanks to my daughters, Kirsten and Susi, for making me proud of their life achievements and also for helping Margot and me overcome difficult situations. I would like to thank all of my friends - there are too many to name - who generously gave me their assistance whenever I needed it. Thanks to all of my employees at Berggasthof Hoherodskopf in Germany and Handke's Cuisine in Columbus, Ohio. They made me successful. I couldn't have made it without them nor could I have served the meals that we did. We never would have achieved the highest Zagat rating - 28 out of 30 points - in the state of Ohio. Last but not least, this never would have happened without three people who gave me the idea of doing it and then getting it done. Nick Versteeg, the producer of all kinds of documentaries, was filming the Canadian Culinary Olympic team in 2012 in Erfurt, Germany. I served as his assistant cameraman, using the smallest camera he could find for me. When I mentioned to him that I wanted him to do some food-related videos for me, his answer was: "Do an eBook with your story, recipes and videos. Get yourself an iPad and start writing." That was easier said than done. I purchased an iPad even though I could hardly handle a computer. I made a rough outline, wrote a chapter and stopped. Then I wrote another chapter and stopped again. This went on and on, and I realized I was getting nowhere. I needed someone to write the story with me. After talking to several people, I couldn't find the right person. That changed last January when I catered a small party for Dr. Hagop Mekhjian. Erika Mitiska and her husband were in attendance, and I asked her if she'd be interested in translating my German English into proper English and doing the writing for me. She was very excited about this opportunity even though I warned her that this was not a small project. Finally, my daughter Susi edited all of the recipes. I cannot tell Nick, Erika and Susi how thankful I am that we completed the project.

What to Expect from this Book

My name is Hartmut Handke, German by birth and an American citizen by choice. I am a semi-retired chef, restaurateur, consultant, and play many roles in the hospitality industry.

I was born in a small town near Dresden, Germany. My father was a school teacher, and my mother was a homemaker and an excellent cook. I had a brother who followed in my footsteps and became a chef. Over the years, a lot of people encouraged me to write a cookbook and I thought that was a big compliment. I considered it, but because I was always busy and short on time - and because the market is flooded with cookbooks - I put this project on the back burner. Until now.

My friend, Nick Versteeg, encouraged me to do this project. So here I am, 76 years old (or young, depending on your point of view) with 59 years of experience in the hospitality industry and - until nine years ago a man who didn't even know how to turn on a computer - writing my experiences in a book.

From my early career as a chef's apprentice until my retirement as a Certified Master Chef and restaurateur, this book explores stories and recipes based on all kinds of ingredients and experiences gathered from nearly 60 years of working and traveling all over the world. I hope you enjoy it. Life is good. Food is fun. Let's live and eat well.

A Divided Family and Country

It was cold and snowing, and we had to walk five miles to our new home.

My earliest childhood memory is perhaps the realization that my father was away at war. My mother worked very hard as an embroiderer to raise my brother and me during the difficult war time when food was scarce and the men were away. In those days, we had very few communication means: my father did not have a phone and sometimes we would go for months without hearing from him.

At the end of World War II in 1945, my father was taken prisoner of war by the Americans in Holland. Germany was divided into four "sectors" - American, English, French and Russian. The Americans released prisoners of war to relatives who lived in any sector except the Russian sector. Because my mother, brother and I still lived in Kamenz, a small village near Dresden located in the Russian sector, my father could not use our address. He remembered that he had some very distant relatives in the small town of Schotten, which is just north of Frankfurt am Main and was in the American sector. He used their address and was released.

So he settled in Schotten, where his relatives provided him with meals and a small cottage in exchange for repairs around their property as well as work on their small farm. Before the war, my father was a teacher, but he was also very handy and could repair and build just about anything.

Once he was organized and settled, he decided it was time to get the family back together. At the end of February 1946, he traveled for three days by train, bus and hitchhiking to Kamenz. Needless to say, we were overjoyed to see him! Since we had not heard from him for many months, we did not even know if he was still alive.

He told my mother to pack up only the most necessary things that we could carry. We were to leave quietly the next evening. This all had to be done very secretly because as a government employee/teacher, my father had been required to be a member of the Party of the Hitler Regime. If the new government of the Russian sector in Germany discovered that he had come home, they would have put him in jail and maybe even deported him to Siberia.

After three days of traveling, we arrived at the railway station in Schotten, our new hometown. Even though I was barely six years old, I still remember that day like it was yesterday. The train pulled into the station around 8 pm. It was cold and snowing, and we had to walk five miles to our new home. I recall that walk vividly. I could see the light of the house where we were going - way out in the country. We walked and walked, and it didn't seem like we ever drew any closer. However, after two hours of walking, we finally made it. This was probably my first lesson in perseverance.

Growing up in the Country: My School Years

We had eggs and every so often on Sundays, a roasted chicken or Hassenpfeffer, a rabbit stew.

I t was the end of February when we arrived in Schotten. The climate in this region of Germany is similar to that of the U.S. Midwest, so we were initially greeted with snowy, chilly weather. Thank goodness spring arrived five weeks later!

Not only was it cold, neither of my parents had a steady income other than a small government stipend. My father continued to work for our relatives, and my mother was a homemaker. She cooked, knitted and sewed clothes for us with whatever fabric she could find. There was not much food in the stores; everything was rationed. Every family received a food card each month that the storekeeper collected when you shopped. The food cards had little tickets on them that you cut off and exchanged for common food ingredients - things like flour and margarine (butter was not available). There was a lot of bartering as well. For example, if you knew that you were not going to use all of your food tickets for the month, you bartered your extra tickets with somebody for something that you could use and the other person could not. A good example was cigarettes. Adults received cigarette tickets so they could buy one pack a week. My parents didn't smoke, so they bartered those tickets for something else. I also remember that my parents traded some of their wedding gifts (towels, linens, sheets and tablecloths) for a seven-day-old baby goat. We raised this goat and eventually had our own milk.

Before we owned the goat, my mother and I walked about 4 miles one way to a nearby village every other evening to get two liters of fresh milk. My mother let the milk rest for 24 hours, then skimmed the cream off the top and used the milk. She carefully rationed the cream to us for a few days. Then on Sundays in the summer, she cooked *Rote Gruetze*, or **Red Grits**, a delicious red berry dessert that she served with whipped cream: a very special dish. As a chef, in later years, I also prepared *Rote Gruetze* and served it with a **Sauce Anglaise** or vanilla sauce.

My mother did not purchase the precious berries for her *Rote Gruetze* during this time of rationing. The area where we lived was wooded and after living there about a year, we knew where to find the best summer berries: raspberries, blackberries, blueberries and tiny wild strawberries. In the fall, we picked elderberries. After we brought home the berries, my mother made not only the delicious *Rote Gruetze*, but also preserves and juices for the winter.

Our second year in Schotten, we leased a small parcel of land (approximately 600 square feet) for a vegetable garden. Here we grew nearly every common vegetable that you can imagine. The vegetable that I remember very well is radishes. My little brother and I could hardly wait until these spicy red root vegetables were ready to harvest. Once they started growing, we checked every so often to see if they were large enough to eat. We wiggled the radishes just a little bit out of the ground, and if they were not ready, we shoved them back into the soil. The problem however, was that these radishes that we had "checked" could not grow anymore. The "pep talk" our father gave us when he discovered what we were up to was not very pleasant.

That same year we also started raising chickens and rabbits, and our lifestyle improved. We had eggs and every so often on Sundays, a roasted chicken or **Hassenpfeffer**, a rabbit stew. I still remember the scrumptious chicken dishes. My mother could make two meals from one chicken. On Saturday mornings, my father killed and butchered a chicken. Then, my mother boiled the whole chicken with vegetables. Once the chicken was tender, she removed it from the broth, added her homemade noodles to the liquid to cook them, and Saturday lunch was ready: chicken noodle soup with vegetables. On Sunday, my mother cut up the chicken, sautéed it in margarine (we still couldn't buy butter) until it was golden brown, and served it with boiled potatoes and vegetables. Two fabulous meals! When times were really good, my mother cooked delicious **Veal Meatballs with Caper Sauce**.

Another meat dish that my mother prepared is **Lamb and Green Bean Stew**. However, she didn't use lamb, but rather mutton - an old lamb, a sheep really. Because mutton has a strong, gamey flavor and aroma, when she cooked it on Saturdays, whole house smelled like lamb.

Although we didn't have meat every day, my mother was a very good cook. She produced some very tasty meals. A typical meatless meal consisted of mashed potatoes served with fruit compote and *Quark*, a Germany dairy product that is similar to a thick yogurt or farmer's cheese. With the diet we consumed, there was no way we could become obese. Also, we climbed trees and played all kinds of games in the woods. Our diet and our lifestyle kept us as thin as beanstalks! But everybody was happy and healthy.

In 1946, when I was six years old, I started first grade. We lived about four miles out of town, and transportation by school bus was unheard of in those days. I had to walk to school. Sadly, I only owned one pair of shoes, a pair of heavy leather boots that I had to save for the winter. The only choice was to go barefoot. Since the road was not paved, I split my big toe open on a sharp stone more than once. Then around the time I entered third grade, my father found a front wheel, a rear wheel, a handlebar, a saddle and a bike frame. He put everything together and - voila! - I had a bicycle with brakes on the rear wheel. He put a bucket behind the saddle, so after school I could go to my parents' friends' homes to collect potato peels, vegetable trimmings and other food scraps to feed our animals. Once in a while, the bucket fell off the carrier. What a mess! But nevertheless, things were improving and we knew little of the world outside our town. We had food, we were healthy, and we were a happy family.

Red Grits
Yields 10 Portions

Ingredients

1½ lbs Fresh or Frozen Unsweetened Berries (strawberries cut in wedges, raspberries, blueberries, blackberries)
4 oz Sugar
1½ cups Water
2 oz Minute Tapioca
½ cup Cold Water
1 oz Raspberry Liqueur, such as Chambord
2 Tbsp Shaved Dark Chocolate, for garnish
10 each Fresh Red Raspberries, for garnish

Method

1. Place the berries, sugar and 1½ cups of water in a pot over high heat and bring to a boil.
2. Meanwhile, combine the Minute Tapioca with ½ cup cold water and allow to bloom for 3 minutes.

3. When the berry mixture begins to boil, stir in the tapioca and water mixture and bring the mixture back to a boil, stirring continuously. Lower the heat to a simmer and cook for 3-4 minutes, stirring frequently, to thoroughly cook the tapioca.

4. Remove from the heat and stir in the raspberry liqueur.

5. Pour into champagne or wine glasses. Chill in a refrigerator for at least 2 hours to allow to set before serving.

To serve

Pour a ¼-inch layer of Di Saronno Sauce Anglaise on top of the chilled Red Grits. Garnish each serving with shaved dark chocolate and 1 fresh raspberry.

Di Saronno Sauce Anglaise
Yields 1 Quart

Ingredients

1 pint Heavy Cream
1 cup Milk
4½ oz Sugar
½ each Vanilla Bean, split lengthwise
1 cup Milk
¾ oz Cornstarch
1 each Egg Yolk
1½ oz Di Saronno liqueur (Amaretto)

Method

1. In a heavy bottomed sauce pot, combine the heavy cream, 1 cup milk and sugar. Scrape the vanilla beans into the mixture and then add the bean. Bring to a boil.
2. Meanwhile, in a small bowl, whisk the cornstarch into the remaining 1 cup milk until smooth. Whisk in the egg yolk.
3. Remove the cream mixture from the heat and allow to cool for 2 minutes.
4. Using a piano wire whip, whisk the egg yolk mixture into the cream mixture. Return the pot to the stove and bring to a boil, whisking constantly to keep the mixture from sticking and burning on the bottom of the pot. Reduce the heat to a simmer and continue to cook, stirring with a rubber spatula (be sure to scrape along the bottom of the pot), until the mixture is thickened and the starch is cooked.
5. Remove from the heat and strain the mixture through a fine sieve (chinois) and into a bowl set into an ice bath. Stir constantly to cool the mixture thoroughly and quickly.
6. Once the Sauce Anglaise is cold, stir in the Amaretto Di Saronno. Cover and refrigerate until ready to serve. Store any leftover sauce, covered and refrigerated for up to 3 days.

Vanilla Sauce Anglaise
Yields 1 Quart

Ingredients

1 pint Heavy Cream
1 cup Milk
4½ oz Sugar
1 Tbsp Vanilla Extract
1 cup Milk
¾ oz Cornstarch
1 each Egg Yolk

Method

1. In a heavy bottomed sauce pot, combine the heavy cream, 1 cup milk, sugar and vanilla extract. Bring to a boil.
2. Meanwhile, in a small bowl, whisk the cornstarch into the remaining 1 cup milk until smooth. Whisk in the egg yolk.
3. Remove the cream mixture from the heat and allow to cool for 2 minutes.
4. Using a piano wire whip, whisk the egg yolk mixture into the cream mixture. Return the pot to the stove and bring to a boil, whisking constantly to keep the mixture from sticking and burning on the bottom of the pot. Reduce the heat to a simmer and continue to cook, stirring with a rubber spatula (be sure to scrape along the bottom of the pot), until the mixture is thickened and the starch is cooked.
5. Remove from the heat and strain the mixture through a fine sieve (chinois) and into a bowl set into an ice bath. Stir constantly to cool the mixture thoroughly and quickly.
6. Cover and refrigerate until ready to serve. Store any leftover sauce, covered and refrigerated for up to 3 days.

Hassenpfeffer (Rabbit Ragout)
Yields 6 Portions

Ingredients

Marinade

1½ cups Large Diced Onion
1½ cups Large Diced Celeriac
1½ cups Large Diced Carrot
8 each Juniper Berries, crushed with the side of a knife
1-2 each Bay Leaves
2 each Whole Cloves
10 each Black Peppercorns, crushed
3 lb Rabbit, cut into 1½ to 2-inch pieces with bones, using the front legs, neck and chest of the animal

Sauce

2 oz Unsalted Butter
1 Tbsp Tomato Paste
2-3 Tbsp All-purpose Flour

To finish

to taste Salt
to taste Freshly Ground Black Pepper
to taste Red Wine
to taste Lemon Juice

Method

1. Prepare the marinade by combining all of the marinade ingredients. Place the rabbit meat in the marinade, cover and refrigerate for 12 hours.
2. Remove the meat from the marinade.
3. Strain the vegetables from the marinade and reserve both the vegetables and the liquid.
4. Place the butter in a heavy duty pot and sear off the rabbit meat.
5. Remove the meat from the pot, set it aside, and add the reserved vegetables to the same pot.
6. Add the tomato paste and caramelize it with the vegetables a little, taking care not to burn it.
7. Add the flour and mix well.
8. Add the reserved marinade liquid and bring to a simmer while stirring.
9. Add the meat and simmer for about one hour until the meat is tender.
10. Remove the meat and place it in a serving dish.
11. Adjust the sauce seasoning as needed with salt, pepper, red wine and lemon juice.
12. Strain the sauce over the meat and serve immediately. Serve with Spaetzle and Braised Red Cabbage.

Veal Meatball with Caper Sauce
(Koenigsberger Klopse mit Kapern Sauce)
Yields 6 Portions

Ingredients

For the cooking liquid
2 quarts Water
1 each Small Onion, rough chopped
1 each Bay Leaf
1 each Celery Stalk
to taste Salt
to taste Freshly Ground Black Pepper

For the meatballs
1 lb Veal Shoulder Trimmings, ground with small die
1 each Small Onion, small diced
¼ cup Whole Milk
1 cup Dried Breadcrumbs
2 each Whole Eggs
to taste Salt
to taste Freshly Ground Black Pepper

Method

1. Place all of the ingredients for the cooking liquid in a large pot and bring to a simmer.
2. Place all of the ingredients for the meatballs in a bowl and mix well.
3. Shape the mixed meat into 2 ½ oz balls and set aside.
4. Place the meatballs in the cooking liquid and simmer for 10 minutes.
5. Remove the meatballs from the cooking liquid and keep warm.
6. Strain the cooking liquid and use for the caper sauce.

To serve

1. Place the meat balls in the caper sauce and serve.
2. Garnish with chopped parsley and serve with boiled potatoes.

Caper Sauce
Yields 1 Serving

Ingredients

½ cup Unsalted Butter
1/3 cup All-purpose Flour
1 quart Cooking Liquid from the meatballs
½ cup Capers
3 Tbsp Liquid from the capers
1 each Egg Yolk
1/3 cup Heavy Cream
to taste Salt
to taste Freshly Ground White Pepper

Method

1. Melt the butter in a small sauce pot. Add the flour and mix well to make a light roux. Whisk in the cooking liquid from the veal meat balls to prepare a veloute sauce. Simmer, whisking occasionally, for ten minutes.
2. Add the capers and caper liquid and cook until heated through.
3. Mix the heavy cream with the egg yolk and fold into the caper sauce. Remove the caper sauce immediately from the heat.

Lamb and Green Bean Stew
(Lamb und Grüne Bohnen Eintopf)
Yields 6 Portions

Ingredients

2 qt Water
2 each Lamb Shanks
2 qt Cold Water
½ each Small Onion, cut in half
1 each Celery Stick, cut in pieces
1 each Medium Carrot, cut in small pieces
2 each Bay Leaves
2 each Fresh Tarragon Sprigs
to taste Salt
to taste Freshly Ground Black Pepper
3 cups Green Beans, cut short
3 cups ¼" Diced Potatoes
1 Tbsp Chopped parsley

Method

1. Put first the first two quarts of water in a pot large enough to fit the 2 lamb shanks, along with the lamb shanks, and make sure the lamb shanks are well covered by the water.
2. Bring to a boil.
3. Remove from the heat. Discard, the water and rinse the lamb shanks; wash the pot.
4. Place the lamb shanks back into the pot and add two quarts of cold water, onion, celery, carrot, bay leaves and tarragon sprigs.
5. Bring to a boil, then cut the heat down to a simmer. The lamb shanks should be well done after cooking for approximately one hour. Remove the shanks from the pot and strain the stock into a clean pot. Discard the vegetables.
6. Add the green beans and potatoes to the stock and cook until tender. In the meantime, cut the meat of the bone of the lamb shank and cut into small bite-sized pieces. Add the stock, beans and potatoes.
7. Ladle in a soup terrine. Sprinkle chopped parsley on top and serve family style.

Moving from the Country to the "City"

My friends and I really enjoyed working on the farms because in addition to the small pay we received, we were also fed excellent, home-cooked meals.

At the end of 1949, my father was reinstated as a teacher and a lot of changes came along with it. First, we had a steady income - not too much, but better than nothing. Second, we moved into an apartment in the school building in Schotten. Schotten was a typical small German town with about 4,500 inhabitants, a hospital, a grammar school through 8th grade, a middle school for trade-bound students, a *Gymnasium* (high school) for university-bound students, some small farms, some food stores and other shops where tradesmen like carpenters and shoemakers sold their goods. It was not unusual at this time for a school teacher to live in the school building, and we were very happy and excited about it.

After completing fourth grade, all students were aptitude tested to determine whether they would attend *Gymnasium* or middle school. Although I passed the test for the *Gymnasium*, I decided, with the approval of my parents, to attend middle school instead. I was more practical and just couldn't see myself going to school for 13 years and then attending the university for another four to six years.

The next six years were much more organized and exciting. During vacation time, I did all kinds of jobs to earn some pocket money. When I was 12, I had a job in a saw mill cutting and bundling firewood. I also collected berries and sold them to a juice company. For three days each summer, I cleaned one kilometer of Schotten's motorcycle race track during the annual races. I worked on a farm to help harvest the grain. My pay for the farm work was two four-week-old roosters, which eventually became two Sunday meals. My friends and I really enjoyed working on the farms because in addition to the small pay we received, we were also fed excellent, home-cooked meals. We especially enjoyed the homemade sausage. We spent the money that we earned on accessories for our bicycles and all kinds of other stuff that boys like. We also saved our money for bicycle tours and overnight stays in youth hostels. Life was good and getting better.

Getting Ready to Start a Career: Leaving Home and Conquering the World

My parents delivered me in the sidecar of the Triumph motorcycle on March 31, 1957 to begin my work in the culinary world.

My six years in middle school were very enjoyable. I was a fairly average student with A's and B's in every subject - except for the C's in shorthand and French. There was a small problem in the 5th grade with my English teacher, who had worked in London for a while as a banker. He thought that, since he spoke English fairly fluently, he was a good teacher. I don't think he liked me too much because every time we had English, I had to leave the classroom after about five minutes and stand in front of the door. He said I interrupted his teaching. This would not have been too awful if our apartment hadn't have been on the same floor as my classroom. Occasionally my mother came out of our apartment and saw me standing there. Naturally she wanted to know what I was doing *outside* the classroom. As an 11 year old, I told her the truth. She then told my father, who was very upset. I was supposed to set a good example for the rest of the class.

Another less-than-ideal situation was that I had my father as a main teacher for the last six years of middle school. This was definitely not an advantage. Whenever I did something that I wasn't supposed to do in other classes, he knew about it before school was out at 1pm. I heard all about it during lunch! But he was a very good educator and we learned a lot from him. Every year, we traveled with him on an educational trip for a week somewhere in Germany, staying in youth hostels and taking hiking tours to castles and other interesting locations. He was the only teacher who did this. I guess the other teachers were too lazy or too worried that something bad might happen.

In tenth grade, about six months before graduation, the nine boys and nine girls in my class more or less knew their plans for the future. Everyone was going to do an apprenticeship. The girls decided that they wanted to be secretaries and nurses. The boys decided to become carpenters, mechanics and masons. I was the only one who wanted to become a chef. In fact, I believe I was the first person from our little town to select this profession. In the following years, quite a few more people followed in my footsteps, including my own brother. To this day people ask me, "Why did you want to be a chef?" Well, my answer is very simple: I wanted to see the world. As a chef, I could do this without ever being unemployed because people always have to eat. Being a chef has allowed my desire to travel to become a reality.

The question now was: Where would I find a place to start my apprenticeship? My father had done some research and came to the conclusion it should (1) be a first class hotel or restaurant; and (2) be located in one of Germany's southern states. The reason for concentrating on southern Germany was that every year the apprentices in this part of the country studied and lived at a community college for six weeks - much like a boarding school. In the north, the apprentices went to a community college one day each week, every week, which was disruptive.

After I mailed about a dozen applications to fine hotels and restaurants in southern Germany, I received about six invitations for interviews. My father, who was the proud owner of a 250cc Triumph motorbike with a sidecar, took me to visit the places that had granted me interviews. At each place, we spent some time with the general manager, then we were shown to the kitchen and introduced to the executive chef. The general manager and the executive chef not only asked me all kinds of questions, but they also wanted to see my school report card. Then the *sous chef* interviewed me. Last but not least, a third-year apprentice showed me around the kitchen - the walk-ins, the freezers and the various stations. At the end, we had a short meeting with the executive chef, who told us that we would know the decision in a few weeks.

It is important to note that in 1957, unemployment in Germany was pretty high and employers had a big selection of applicants for open positions. But as I recall, I received three positive answers. Now it was up to me (and my father) to make a decision. We chose Baden-Baden's Hotel Europaeischer Hof, a property which belonged to the Steigenberger Hotel Group in Germany. I think my father really liked the chef because he was originally from East Prussia (my father was born in Silesia, which shares a border with East Prussia). Both were disciplinarians, and I eventually discovered that this would guarantee an excellent and highly-disciplined education for Handke junior.

At the end of March 1957, I graduated from middle school. The first day of my apprenticeship was April 1, so my parents delivered me in the sidecar of the Triumph motorcycle on March 31, 1957 to begin my work in the culinary world.

Baden-Baden

Given its rich history, famous spas and fashionable horse racing, Baden-Baden is very well known for its high gastronomic standard.

Baden-Baden is called the grand old lady of German spas. Its reputation of having spas with healthy and healing water that you can drink or bath in dates back more than 200 years. The spas have been frequented by emperors, kings, counts and other wealthy people from all around the world. People visit Baden-Baden in the spring, summer and fall to take care of their well-being, while also enjoying the city and its surrounding area. It is a place to see and be seen.

Beautiful hotels and private villas are situated along the little Oos River, which runs right through the center of town. Historic hotels built in the grand old style like Brenner's Park Hotel, Hotel Europaeischer Hof, Hotel Bellevue, Hotel Badischer Hof and Hotel Hirsch are all first-class establishments. The *Kurhaus* was and remains the center of many social activities. It is the home of Baden-Baden's casino, which is referred to as the mother of Monte Carlo's casino. Next to the *Kurhaus* is the theater, an intimate setting for plays, musicals and operas. On the other side of the *Kurhaus* is the *Trinkhalle*, or pump house, an impressive building with a large covered promenade. Here, you can sip a cup of the healing water while strolling the promenade.

In the city's center are two public spas, the older Friedrichsbad and the newer Caracalla. These spas' pools are spring-fed by water that comes out of the ground at approximately 130 degrees Fahrenheit. Since the water is cooled slightly, it is very pleasant to swim or even just sit in it. At both locations you also can enjoy all kinds of saunas, steam baths and massages.

Just outside Baden-Baden in the small village of Iffezheim is a horse-racing track, where the famous *Rennwoche*, or race week, events are attended by Europe's high society every year for one week in August.

Given its rich history, famous spas and fashionable horse racing, Baden-Baden is very well known for its high gastronomic standard. One of my personal favorites from the area is **Spaetzle**.

As a 17-year-old boy from a small town like Schotten, Baden-Baden was very impressive and overwhelming to me. The hotel provided me - and three other apprentices - with room and board, which meant that the four of us shared one room that was just big enough for four beds and two small closets. My monthly salary was 20 German marks for the first year, 40 marks for the second year and 60 marks for the third year.

April 1, my first day in the kitchen, the executive chef decided that I should start at the pastry station. My 35-year-old supervisor, Walter Werker, was a master pastry chef and a master baker from Cologne. He was a very understanding and patient teacher, and a super person to work for. He took me under his wing and showed me where I would find everything. He explained the day-to-day operations and what the executive chef expected from us. Overall, he taught me a lot, and I strove to learn as much as I could from him. We produced all kinds of tortes, cakes, petit fours, cookies and desserts for the a la carte menu. After six months, I was the most highly-trained pastry apprentice in our kitchen. When the pastry chef was off, I was in charge of the shop.

On the eve of one of his days off, Chef Werker told me to make some *Piped Butter Cookies* the next day since we were running low. He knew I was able to do this. We always made three different shapes: round, straight and question marks. We used a pastry bag with a star tube to pipe the cookies, all precisely the same size and shape, onto baking sheets in one long line. On each baking sheet there was room for about 100 pieces.

I worked a split shift, from 8:30am until 2:30pm with two hours of free time followed by work again from 4:30pm until about 10pm. On this particular day, I was alone and I had all kinds of things to do for the lunch service, including preparing the daily home-made ice cream. Therefore, since dinner service didn't start until 6:00pm, I decided to make the cookies right after I returned from my free time. I thought this was an excellent plan. As soon as I arrived in the pastry shop, I prepared the cookie dough and piped the three different shapes onto three baking sheets. The oven was ready, so I put one sheet in right away. After about 15 minutes, the cookies would be a beautiful golden brown. However, just to be sure that everything was going well, it was best to look in the oven at least once during those 15 minutes. Something must have distracted me because I forgot to check the cookies. As a matter of fact, I completely forgot that the cookies were in the oven until I realized that there was a light burned smell in the air. Trouble, trouble, trouble.

The kitchen was approximately 35 yards long with the pastry shop on one end and the *garde manger*, or pantry kitchen, on the opposite side. I glanced quickly to the other end of the kitchen, where I saw the chef talking to the *chef garde manger*, or pantry chef. Now, I had to spring into action. I pulled the baking sheet with the very dark brown cookies out of the oven, scraped the cookies into a large sink, turned the water on full stream, demolished the cookies with a large wire whip and prayed that everything would disappear down the drain. It worked! Unfortunately, though, some of the burned cookie odor must have traveled beyond the pastry shop because the chef at the other end of the kitchen lifted his head, inhaled deeply through his nose, and exclaimed: "Something is burning!" It did not take him long to figure out that something was happening in the pastry shop. When he asked me if I had burned anything, I said: "No, not that I know of." He walked around the pastry shop, sniffing and trying to determine what had happened. Now the sink was white porcelain, and wouldn't you know it, in the corners there were still some dark cookie crumbs, which he noticed immediately. Before I even knew what was happening, he turned and slapped me across the face. He also canceled my afternoon free time for the next two weeks. Instead, for these two hours every day, I had to scrub the walk-in cooler and freezer, clean the trout basin in the basement, peel buckets full of potatoes, clean vegetables for every station, clean the pastry shop from top to bottom and a lot of other things.

The punishment was tough and I was miserable. I began to wonder if it was really worthwhile to continue to train to become a chef. However, I didn't dare to complain to my parents because I knew I was wrong anyway. They were happy that I had a job and was learning a profession under an excellent chef in a five-star property. So, I persevered and completed the three years. I consider this my first big accomplishment.

Overall, the time I spent there in training was a wonderful experience. The most exciting story from my time in Baden-Baden occurred just three months prior to the end of my apprenticeship in 1960, during the *Fasching* or carnival (similar to Mardi Gras) season. This season begins on a Thursday with the *Altweiberfastnacht*, or Old Women's Festival, and ends on Ash Wednesday at 2am. Many festivals take place during *Fasching*, including balls and dances in different venues in the city. Everybody - including the chefs and apprentices - celebrated and had a great time. It was here, on one of the last days of Fasching in 1960, I met Margot, my future wife.

After some time, Margot, who lived in a suburb of Baden-Baden called Lichtenthal, introduced me to her parents since they wanted to know what kind of a fellow she was dating. Her father was a typesetter at the local newspaper and her mother was a homemaker. I was invited for lunch. Margot's mother cooked **Eingemachtes Kalbfleisch**, or *Blanquette de Veau* - which is like a veal fricassee.

The meal was excellent and I complimented her on it. I wasn't trying to earn points; it was really delicious. Her father opened a bottle of Riesling wine from the Pfalz region. It seemed that they liked me and I was accepted. On my next visit, her mother made Leberspaetzle, or **Liver Spaetzle**, the traditional way, cutting the noodles from a board and then boiling them in water. She then sautéed them in a skillet with caramelized onions. She served the Spaetzle with a tossed green salad. In those days, we always consumed hot meals for lunch. At dinner, Margot's mother served cold cuts that she called *Vesper*. She went to the butcher and picked the best local sausage she could find. These were memorable meals. Years later, after we had moved away and came back to visit, her mother remembered my favorite meals and prepared them for me. Margot and I got married five years later, and have been together ever since - more than 50 years! Margot always tells me that if you are married to a chef, it counts double. But that is another story.

Spaetzle
Yields 10 Portions

Ingredients

17 oz All-purpose Flour
6-7 each Eggs, depending on size
1 teaspoon Salt
to taste Fresh Ground White Pepper
3 Tbsp Unsalted Butter

Method

1. In the old times you would put all of the ingredients in a bowl and mix them into a dough. Then you would beat this dough with the inside of your hand until you created bubbles. Today, you can take advantage of the Kitchen Aid mixer. Put all of the ingredients into a Kitchen Aid bowl, and using the paddle run the mixer at medium speed for approximately 5 minutes.

2. Once the dough is done, you can use a Spätzle board and scrape small julienne of dough into lightly salted boiling water with a palette knife or you can use a Spätzle press and push the dough through the holes.

3. Once the Spätzle are floating on top of the water, lift them out of the water and put them in a bowl with ice cold water. Then pour the Spätzle through a colander to drain them.

4. Place the butter in a skillet and add the spätzle and sautée them together. Spätzle are used in the Black Forest region of Germany as a side component to a lot of meat dishes.

5. There are a lot of other Spätzle variations, like Spätzle geschmälzt, saure Spätzle, Leber Spätzle or Käse-Spätzle.

Piped Butter Cookies
Yields about 45 cookies

Ingredients

10¾ oz Unsalted butter
9 oz Confectionary Sugar
4½ oz Cornstarch
1½ cup Milk
1 pinch Salt
1 tsp Vanilla Extract
½ each Lemon, Peel Grated with a Microplane
17¾ oz All-purpose Flour

Method

1. Brush three ½-sized sheet pans (cookie sheets) with butter or cover them with parchment paper or Silpats.
2. Preheat the oven to 370 degrees F.
3. Put the butter, confectionary sugar and cornstarch in a Kitchen Aid bowl. Using the paddle, mix well until the mixture is smooth but not foamy.
4. Add the milk and mix a little more with the paddle.
5. Add the salt, vanilla extract and grated lemon peel.
6. Fold in the flour.
7. In case the dough is too stiff, add some more milk as needed.
8. Fill the dough into a pastry bag with a #8 star tip. Pipe on the sheet pans in any shape you desire.
9. Place in the oven and bake for approximately for 12 minutes until light brown.

Blanquette De Veau
(Engelegtes Kalbfleish)
Yields 10 Portions

Ingredients

3 lb Veal (breast or shoulder), cut into 1-inch cubes
Cold Water for parboiling and washing the veal
2 qt White Stock or Water
1 each Bouquet Garni
    (1 Carrot, 1 Celery Stick, ¼ Onion, ½ Leek, 2 sprigs Fresh Thyme, 1 Bay Leaf)
1 Tbsp Salt
20 each Pearl Onions, poached
20 each Small Button Mushrooms, poached
2 oz Clarified (unsalted) Butter
2 oz All-Purpose Flour
½ cup Heavy Cream
4 each Egg Yolks
few drops Fresh Lemon Juice
to taste Salt and Ground White Pepper
pinch Ground Cayenne Pepper

Method

1. Place the veal cubes in a pot and cover with cold water. Bring to a boil.
2. Remove from heat and wash the veal cubes with more cold water, removing all small particles. Set the washed veal cubes aside and wash the pot well to thoroughly clean it.
3. Add 2 quarts white stock or water to the pot. Add the washed meat, bouquet garni and 1 tablespoon salt.
4. Bring to a simmer and cook for 1½ hours, until the meat is just tender.
5. Drain the veal and reserve the cooking liquid. Discard the bouquet garni. Place the meat in a clean pot along with the pearl onions and button mushrooms. Keep warm.
6. Prepare a Sauce Veloute by first preparing a white (blonde) roux: in a separate pot over medium-high heat, whisk together the clarified butter and flour and cook for 1 minute – whisking constantly and taking care not to allow the roux to darken at all.
7. Immediately whisk 3 pints of the cooking liquid into the roux. Bring to just a boil while whisking constantly, then lower the heat and simmer gently, whisking frequently, for 15 minutes.
8. Prepare the liaison: in a bowl, whisk together the egg yolks and heavy cream. Whisk in the lemon juice. Whisk the egg mixture into the sauce and then remove the sauce from the heat. Season the sauce to taste with salt, pepper and a pinch of cayenne.
9. Set a fine sieve (chinois) into the pot containing the meat and vegetables. Strain the sauce through the chinois and into the pot over the meat, onions and mushrooms. Place the pot over low heat and cook gently, just to reheat. Do not boil.
10. Serve with tourneed parsley potatoes or rice pilaf.

Liver Spaetzle
Yields 6-8 portions

Ingredients

6-½ oz All-purpose Flour
6-½ oz Beef Liver, run twice through the fine die of the meat grinder
2 each Eggs
to taste Salt
to taste Freshly Ground White pepper
pinch Dried Marjoram Flakes
3 Tbsp Fine Chopped Parsley
3 Tbsp Unsalted Butter

Method

1. In the old times you would put all of the ingredients in a bowl and mix them into a dough. Then you would beat this dough with the inside of your hand until you created bubbles. Today, you can take advantage of the Kitchen Aid. Put all of the ingredients in the bowl, and using the paddle run the Kitchen Aid at medium speed for approximately 5 minutes.
2. Once the dough is done, you can use a spaetzle board and scrape the small juliennes of dough into lightly salted boiling water, or you can use a spaetzle press and push them through the holes.
3. Once the spaetzle are floating on top of the water, take them out of the water and put them in a bowl with ice cold water. Then pour the spaetzle into a colander to drain.
4. In the meantime, place the butter and onions in a skillet. When the onions are slightly caramelized add the spaetzle and reheat them. Serve with a green salad.

School Time!

First-year apprentices went to The Hotel Zum Mohren.

As I mentioned before, in the state of Baden-Wuerttemberg apprentices attend six weeks of community college once a year on a small island called Reichenau in Lake Constance. On Reichenau there were two hotels: Hotel Zum Mohren and Hotel Loechnerhaus, which were leased by the Hotel and Restaurant Association to be used as boarding schools from November 1 through April 1. Every six weeks a group of hospitality apprentices, including chefs, cooks, waiters and other hospitality people, arrived there from the state of Baden-Wuerttemberg. As you can imagine, 60 male apprentices from the hospitality industry under one roof is quiet an exciting affair.

Our teachers were experienced executive chefs and *maitres d*'s from large hotels that were closed during the winter. The school was run like a military school with very precise rules and regulations. In our classroom sessions, we learned things like dining room and kitchen manners, food and beverage training and mathematics (so we could double or triple our recipes, for example). It was all theory - no hands-on sessions. Saturdays we only had classroom sessions until noon and then the weekend started. Students, who lived nearby and had the financial means, went home; the rest stayed at the school.

First-year apprentices went to The Hotel Zum Mohren. Each room accommodated four students. The food was decent, but nothing special. The owner's wife cooked all of the meals, and we all thought that she maybe didn't complete a three-year culinary apprenticeship!

Now, the Hotel Loechnerhaus was quite a different story. Here, the rooms were occupied by only two students. They had an executive chef, a couple *commis chefs*, or junior chefs and some support from the "on duty students." Therefore, the food was great! The *Wienerschnitzel* was especially excellent.

I enjoyed going to school again. The escape from my regular workplace for six weeks was welcomed. I found that I could really concentrate on studying. Also, I met new people and made new friends. Even though we were there in the wintertime when Lake Constance was frozen, the area was very scenic. On top of all of this, my workplace paid for room and board and travel expenses. Overall it was a great experience.

Switzerland

One of the winter highlights was when the hotel rented six horse-drawn sleighs to take 30 guests from the hotel to a restaurant just three miles outside of Grindelwald for a Cheese Fondue party.

After I finished my apprenticeship and passed the test to become a *Commis de Cuisine*, or junior chef, I left the Hotel Europäischer Hof on March 31, 1960. I was ready to see the world. I had sent an application to the Holland America Line, and was accepted as a *Commis de Cuisine* for the ship, *Maasdam*. In the 1960s, ships were not used for cruises, but mainly for Atlantic crossings. A round-trip from Rotterdam, Netherlands to New York took approximately 21 days with stops in Le Havre, France; Southampton, England; and Cobh, Ireland.

In the dining car on the train to Rotterdam, before my first Atlantic crossing, I met a gentleman who was a chef from Switzerland. During our conversation, I told him that I was on my way to see the world. He thought that working on a ship was not a good idea and recommended that I work in Switzerland instead. Now, Switzerland was not exactly my idea of seeing the world since it was right next to Germany - just a couple hours away by train or car. But before we parted ways, he gave me his address and told me that if I ever wanted to come to Switzerland, I should contact him and he could get me a job.

After just three days on the ship working as *commis entremetier,* or vegetable cook, peeling potatoes and cleaning vegetables for 800 people, I decided that I hadn't done a three-year fine-dining apprenticeship for this. I wrote a letter to my new friend in Switzerland and accepted his offer to find me a job. As soon as we landed in New York, I mailed the letter to him. Nine days later in Rotterdam, I received his reply offering a position in Switzerland at the Kulm Hotel Alpenruhe in Wengen in the Bernese Oberland.

The Kulm Hotel Alpenruhe is a 30-room, family-owned and operated hotel. *"Kulm"* means that this hotel is located at the highest altitude of all of the hotels in the village. Here, I was the *chef de cuisine*, or the main chef. Because the other employees came for the season from Italy, I was the only German-speaking person in the hotel - other than the owners. Language was not a problem, though, as the kitchen helpers learned some German and I picked up some Italian. The working hours were good: I was in charge of lunch and dinner. Since we only cooked for our house guests, we were done by 8pm. The salary was great - especially in comparison to the 60 meager marks I earned monthly during the last year of my apprenticeship. Whenever I needed money, I just went to the office and asked for an advance.

I spent my money in the evenings. The larger hotels in Wengen had very nice bars that I visited after work to socialize with friends. My favorite drink was Queen Anne Scotch with milk. Life was good and I lived like a king.

Now, my father had encouraged me to save some money. However, at the end of August the season in Wengen was over, and I had saved nothing. I had to remedy this situation before I returned home. So, I found a job in a small hotel near Zug for seven weeks, filling in for the chef, who had to fulfill his army duty. I saved every penny that I earned there. When I returned home, I was in good shape financially and my father was very proud of me.

After being home for a couple weeks, I received a not-so-pleasant letter from the German government. They ordered me to report for a physical, after which they would draft me into the German army. I would have been required to do a four-month boot camp followed most likely by 18 months spent in the kitchen, cooking for my fellow soldiers and earning 60 marks a month.

Of course this did not fit into my plans at all! I had already applied to the Holland America Line for a position as a cook aboard the SS Rotterdam, which was scheduled for a world cruise. When I told the government employees at the drafting station about my situation, they assured me that as long as I worked with a shipping line, I was excused from the draft. Unfortunately, since the Holland America Line already had enough chefs for their world cruise, I received a rejection letter. Well, what now? My next best plan seemed to be: Get out of Germany. I successfully landed a job in Zweisimmen, Switzerland at the Hotel Bristol-Terminus opposite the railway station for the winter. It was nothing special, but definitely better than the draft.

The following summer and winter seasons, I continued working in Switzerland at the Hotel Adler in Grindelwald, a little village located in the Bernese Oberland right below the Jungfrau, Eiger Northface and Moench mountains. It was a very picturesque, beautiful countryside, ideal for hiking in the summertime and for skiing and ice skating in the winter.

One of the winter highlights was when the hotel rented six horse-drawn sleighs to take 30 guests from the hotel to a restaurant just three miles outside of Grindelwald for a ***Cheese Fondue*** party. The hotel sent a chef and two waiters as well as an accordion player for entertainment. There, the chef cooked fondue in pottery casserole dishes. The waiter placed the fondue in the middle of each round table of six to eight people. Each guest had a long, two-pronged fork and each table had a basket of French bread cubes. The guests placed a piece of bread on the fork, dipped it in the cheese fondue and ate it. A Swiss white wine called *Fendant* was served with the fondue. Now, here comes the kicker. If someone lost his bread cube in the fondue pot, he had to order a round of *Eau de Vie*, or brandy, for the entire table. These fondue evenings became very entertaining!

When we weren't serving fondue, our customers other favorite dishes included ***Sliced Veal Zurich Style*** and ***Roesti Potatoes***.

Between seasons, I returned to the Holland America Line for two three-week trips to Montreal, Canada and back to Rotterdam, Netherlands. During the last trip to Montreal, I decided that maybe it was time to leave Europe and live overseas. I met with the Queen Elizabeth Hotel's executive chef, Albert Schnell, and inquired about the possibility of working there. He replied that if I obtained an immigration visa, then he would have a job for me.

However, there was now a small "problem" to be considered. Two years earlier, Margot and I became engaged. She had always lived at home and, except for some vacations, had never lived anywhere other than in Baden-Baden. It took a whole lot of talking to convince her - and then her parents - that it would be a fabulous idea to immigrate to Canada. Ultimately, I succeeded. So, on May 15, 1962 we boarded an airplane in Frankfurt, Germany; connected in Brussels, Belgium; and then flew on a small DC-7 (flying by jet was very expensive) for nearly 15 hours to Montreal. Canada, here we come! But that is another story.

Cheese Fondue
Yields 6 Portions

Ingredients

1 clove Garlic
12-14 oz Dry Swiss White Wine
12 oz Gruyere cheese, grated
12 oz Emmentaler cheese, grated
½ oz Cornstarch
¾ oz Kirschwasser
pinch Ground White Pepper
pinch Grated Nutmeg
1½ lb Crusty French Bread, cut into 1-inch cubes

Method

1. Rub the entire inside of the fondue pot with the garlic clove.
2. Pour the white wine into the pot and bring nearly to a boil.
3. Add the grated cheeses, stirring continuously with a wooden spoon.
4. Mix the cornstarch together with the kirschwasser.
5. When the cheese mixture almost reaches the boiling point, stir in the cornstarch/
kirschwasser mixture and continue stirring, adding a little white pepper and grated nutmeg.
6. Transfer the fondue pot to a spirit burner that can be regulated.
7. Serve the bread separately in a basket or serving dish.
8. Using a fork, dip the bread into the fondue and remember to stir the fondue with each
piece. The fondue should be kept at a simmer whilst eating. In case the fondue gets too

Sliced Veal Zurich Style
(Zuricher Kalbsgeschnetzeltes)
Yields 6 Portions

Ingredients

16 oz Veal, preferably loin or tenderloin, thinly sliced by hand
10 oz Veal Kidneys, thinly sliced by hand
to season Salt
to season Freshly Ground White Pepper
3 oz Unsalted Butter
3 oz Shallots, finely diced
5 oz Button Mushrooms, thinly sliced
to taste Salt
to taste Freshly Ground White Pepper
pinch Finely Chopped Fresh Basil
3½ oz White Wine
3½ oz Brown Stock
2 Tbsp Beurre Manie (mixture of equal parts butter and flour)
7 oz Heavy Cream
Thinly Sliced Zest of ¼ Lemon
1½ Tbsp Chopped Fresh Parsley

Method

1. Season the veal and kidney slices with salt and pepper and quickly sauté in butter one at a time. Remove from the pan and keep hot.
2. Sweat the shallots and mushrooms and season with salt, pepper and fresh basil.
3. Deglaze the pan with white wine, add the brown stock and simmer for 5 minutes.
4. Remove the mushrooms with a slotted spoon. Thicken the sauce with the Buerre Manie and strain.
5. Add the heavy cream, then the meat and mushrooms, stirring gently. Reheat, but do not boil.
6. Transfer to a serving dish and sprinkle with parsley. Serve with Roesti or Spaetzle.

Roesti from Zurich
(Zuricher Roesti)
Yields 6 Portions

Ingredients

3 oz Diced Onions
2 oz Julienne Bacon
2 oz Butter
32 oz Peeled Raw Potatoes, roughly grated with a multi-grater using large holes
to taste Salt
to taste Freshly Ground Black Pepper
1 Tbsp Short-cut Fresh Chives
1 Tbsp Chopped Fresh Parsley

Method

1. Sweat the onions, bacon and butter in a heavy duty skillet. Add the potatoes and spread over the bottom of the skillet. Season with salt and pepper and sprinkle some of the herbs on top.
2. When the potatoes are golden brown on the bottom, flip them over and cook until the other side is golden brown as well. By this time, the potatoes should be cooked through.
3. Remove the roesti from the skillet and put on a serving plate. Cut into 6 wedges. Sprinkle with the remaining herbs.

Immigrating to Montreal, Canada

Several times in the fall we traveled north of Montreal to the Laurentian Mountains, where the colors of the maple tree leaves where absolutely beautiful.

When we finally landed in Montreal, it was 2pm. We had our papers in order, so the immigration line at the airport was no problem. Customs, however, was a different story. They wanted to know why I had so many knives in my luggage. It took me quite a while to convince them that they were simply the tools of my trade.

There were two primary reasons that I wanted to work in Montreal. First, I wanted to see the world. Second, I wanted to learn English. Well, Montreal is a wonderful city, and it was really exciting to live there. But, learning English was a different story. Montreal is located in the province of Quebec, where the citizens speak French. In the main kitchen of the Queen Elizabeth Hotel, of the 125 cooks and chefs, 100 were Swiss, German and Austrian and 25 were French Canadian. Guess what language we spoke in the kitchen? German! Eventually even the French Canadians could speak German.

The Queen Elizabeth Hotel, built in 1958, was the headquarters and training center for Hilton International. It was a fantastic new hotel with two great restaurants, the Bonaventure and the Beaver Club and a banquet facility for up to 4,000 guests. Both the corporate executive chef, John Schaerer, and the executive chef, Albert Schnell, were Swiss and excellent culinarians. I became *Commis Saucier and Poissonier*, or assistant sauce chef and fish chef, after my arrival. In this role, I became very adept at preparing luscious lobster dishes like **Lobster Thermidor** and **Lobster Soufflé**.

My work from 3:00pm-11:30pm, five days a week earned a monthly salary of about 250 Canadian dollars. For lunch and dinner, we had a chef's table on the days we worked. But on our days off, we had to provide our own meals. I rented a room from a retired Swiss chef for $12.50 a week, and the daily round-trip bus fare was 50 cents. After paying the expenses, I did not have a lot of spending money and saving money was extremely difficult. Once a month, we splurged on a couple of Labatt beers at the Hofbräuhaus on Bleury Street.

When we first arrived in Canada, Margot did not speak any English, which limited her career options. In Germany she was an accomplished secretary at an architectural firm. In Canada, she accepted a nanny job for two children. She also did some light housekeeping, laundry and ironing for the family, who in turn provided her with free room and board along with a monthly salary of $65.

We tried to get our days off together so we could tour Montreal by bus and on foot. Once in a while, one of my more financially-established colleagues with a used car took us for an outing in the countryside. Several times in the fall we traveled north of Montreal to the Laurentian Mountains, where the colors of the maple tree leaves where absolutely beautiful. Unfortunately, the fall in this part of Canada is very short. When I stepped out of the hotel on October 10, I was surprised to see that the first snow had already arrived. On this particular evening as I was walking home on St. Catherine Street, a passing bus splashed me with a snowy slush from head to toe. I began to wonder whether it was a good idea to spend the winter in Canada.

At the Queen Elizabeth I talked to one of the senior chefs, who had spent some time in the Bahamas. He raved about the islands, admitting that the only reason that he had returned to Canada was his family. Subsequently, I sent my resume to several hotels in Nassau, and received an offer from the British Colonial Hotel. I gave the Queen Elizabeth Hotel two weeks' notice and Margot resigned from her job. We bought two round-trip tickets to the Bahamas with a stopover in New York City.

Just three days prior our departure, the chef from Nassau called and told me that since his business was absolutely flat because of the Bay of Pigs situation in Cuba, he could not employ me. Margot and I were fairly fearless in those days, so I told him that we would tour New York City for a few days anyway. We flew to NYC and checked into *The Wentworth Hotel* on 47th Street. We saw more of the city this time than any other visit. We walked from 2nd Street to 86th Street and from 1st Avenue to 9th Avenue. We ate at delis. For example, dinner consisted of one sandwich with an extra roll and a bottle of pop for about $2.75. I called the chef in Nassau every day. Finally on the fourth day he said that business had improved again and that I could come. This was just in the nick of time, since we were running out of cash. In five days, we had spent $65 for accommodations, food and entertainment. When we boarded the Pan American flight to Nassau, we had $10 between us. But we were on our way to the sunny Bahamas!

Lobster Thermidor
Yields 2 Portions

Ingredients

1 each 2½ lb Lobster
2 quarts Water
1 each Celery Stalk, cut into 2"pieces
1 each Small Onion, peeled and cut in quarters
to taste Salt
8 each Black Peppercorns
1 each Bay Leaf
1 each 2½ lb Lobster
¾ cup White Wine
¾ cup Lobster Stock (use Minor's lobster base to prepare)
1 each Small Shallot, small diced
2 stems Fresh Tarragon, broken up
¾ cup Lobster Veloute
¼ cup Heavy Cream
2 each Egg Yolk
1 tsp Colman's Mustard Powder
to taste Salt and White Pepper
2 oz Grated Parmesan Cheese

Method

1. Prepare the poaching liquid for the lobster by bringing the water, celery, onion, salt black peppercorns and bay leaf to a boil.
2. When the poaching liquid is boiling, add the lobster and cook for 9 minutes. Remove the lobster from the poaching liquid and allow to cool.
3. Split the lobster in half and remove the claws and knuckles from the body. Remove the meat from the lobster body, claws and knuckles and cut into medium dice. Save the two half lobster shells.
4. Put the white wine, lobster stock, diced shallots and tarragon in a small sauce pot and cook until "sec," meaning almost dry with hardly any liquid left.
5. Add the lobster veloute and bring back to a simmer. Strain through a fine mesh sieve and remove from the heat.
6. Mix the heavy cream and egg yolks together and fold into the lobster veloute.
7. Add the ground mustard and season with salt and white pepper to taste.
8. Fold in the lobster meat and half of the grated Parmesan cheese. Fill the two half empty lobster shells and sprinkle the rest of the Parmesan cheese on top.
9. Place on the filled lobster shells on a sheet pan and put in a 425 degrees F preheated oven.
10. When the cheese turns golden brown, remove from the oven and place the lobster on two warm plates. Serve immediately.

Lobster Soufflé

Ingredients

4 Tbsp Unsalted Butter
4 Tbsp All-purpose Flour
3/4 cup Lobster Broth
3/4 cup Heavy Cream
1¼ cup Lobster Meat, diced small
to taste Sea Salt and White Pepper
pinch Ground Cayenne Pepper
2 each Egg Yolks
6 each Egg Whites
1 oz Unsalted Butter (for buttering the soufflé dishes)

Method

1. Make a roux; melt 4 tablespoons butter in a sauce pot and add the flour; mix well with a wooden spoon and cook for 1-2 minutes.
2. Heat the lobster broth and whisk into the roux; bring everything to a boil and cook for 5 minutes.
3. Place the heavy cream in a small pot and bring to almost boiling. While constantly stirring, add the heavy cream to the above. Continue stirring and cook for 5 minutes.
4. Remove from the heat and fold in the diced lobster meat.
5. Season to taste with salt, pepper and cayenne pepper.
6. Temper the egg yolks, one at a time, into the béchamel (that's what it's called now).
7. Beat the egg whites until they are stiff, then fold them into the béchamel/lobster mixture in three additions.
8. Fill the finished soufflé mixture into well buttered soufflé dishes and bake in a preheated oven at 375 degrees F until golden brown on top, for 20-45 minutes depending on the size of the dishes.

Welcome to the Warm and Sunny Bahamas!

In some of the bars in the area known as "over the hills" where the locals lived, we could buy a whole bottle of rum and a mixer that the bartender served with an ice block in a deep bowl, an ice pick and glasses.

Around 2pm our Pan Am clipper touched down at the Nassau International Airport. When the doors of the plane opened, we experienced a tropical climate for the first time in our lives! We cleared immigration by telling them we planned to stay two weeks. We showed them our return tickets to Montreal, and they were satisfied. We sailed through customs too, since we didn't have anything to declare. (Customs was very relaxed, and no one found the knives in my bags this time.) The hotel sent a driver to pick up us, and after a pleasant 25-minute ride, we arrived downtown at the British Colonial Hotel, an imposing pink palace.

Shortly after our arrival, I was introduced to the chef, who explained that the hotel provided room and board for me, but not for Margot. We found a bed and breakfast across the street with an available room. Thankfully they didn't ask for a deposit or credit card because we didn't have either. After I ate dinner at the hotel (and snuck out a little sandwich for Margot), we explored Nassau.

In the Bahamas in the early 1960's, the tourists were mostly well-to-do Americans or Canadians. Most owned houses or apartments on the islands, while some stayed at hotels. Some even brought their own cars and chauffeurs and maids. The majority of them stayed on the islands for the whole winter season - from right after Christmas until Easter. The total number of tourists was still relatively small. High-volume tourism, as we know it today, was not yet common in the Bahamas.

The day after we arrived, I started my job. I worked a split shift for lunch and dinner with a couple hours of free time in the afternoon. This kitchen was completely different from what I was accustomed to. First, it was not terribly clean. Second, all of the pots and pans were very old and not one of them had a flat bottom - they all looked like woks! Finally, I saw quite a few big cockroaches running around. I convinced myself that it is good to see something new.

Before I left Montreal, the senior chef, Joe Kowalski, asked me to visit one of his friends, Manfred Boll, who was the executive chef at Cable Beach's *Nassau*

Beach Hotel, the newest hotel on the Island. Manfred was a few years older than I and was originally from Stuttgart, Germany. So after a few days, I hitchhiked to the *Nassau Beach Hotel* to meet him. I found Manfred in his kitchen office. After I passed along greetings from Joe in Montreal, we started a conversation. He asked how long I had already been on the island, where I worked and whether I liked it. In my response, I mentioned that I was not terribly excited about the *British Colonial Hotel*. Then, to my surprise, he asked me whether I was interested in working for him. Of course I was very interested, but I wasn't sure whether I could resign from my other job so soon. He advised me to wait until after I was paid on Saturday and then talk to the chef. That Saturday evening after I cashed my check, I told the chef that I really didn't like his kitchen and that I wanted to leave. To my surprise, he told me he understood. I finished at the *British Colonial* after dinner Saturday night, and started working at the *Nassau Beach Hotel* on Sunday afternoon at 2:30pm. Since I had a paycheck, our cash flow improved tremendously.

For the next several months, we settled into island life, which was definitely different from Canadian life. We made new friends. We started to speak English with a Bahamian accent. On our days off, we enjoyed the beach, where we went spear fishing for lobster, grouper, snapper, yellow tail and other species. The culinary brigade at the hotel was - with the exception of some Bahamians - German, Swiss, French and a Haitian butcher.

We worked six days a week from 2:30pm until 10:00pm. Most evenings after work, we met with other colleagues in one of our favorite bars for beer or cocktails. Beverages were very cheap on the island. A 24-bottle case of beer was $5.60. Rum, gin and vodka were about $1.20 for a fifth. The mix was actually more expensive than the booze. In some of the bars in the area known as "over the hills" where the locals lived, we could buy a whole bottle of rum and a mixer that the bartender served with an ice block in a deep bowl, an ice pick and glasses: a nifty make-your-own beverage kit. Many times we partied all night, driving home just as the sun was coming up and the fishing boats were returning to the harbor.

After six months on the island, Margot found a job as the manager of a liquor store. Liquor was big business in Nassau at that time because every visitor could purchase five bottles and take them home on the airplane duty free. Nearly everyone took advantage of this excellent deal. Margot was paid a base salary with a commission: three percent for top-shelf sales, two percent for call sales and one percent for all well-liquor sales. Her earnings were so good that, during the season, she made more money than I did.

We purchased a little VW Beetle that I drove a little too fast. Occasionally, I found myself in an "interview" with a police officer. But I had a trick up my sleeve for such situations. When the motorcycle stopped me, I handed the cop my driver's license booklet in which I always had a five-pound bill. When the policemen returned my license, the money was always gone. Then, he *warned* me to "be more careful next time." If I had actually received a ticket, I would have had to go to court. Since hard-working chefs didn't have time to go to court, a local police officer, Mr. Roll, attended for us. My tickets alone could have been a full-time job for him. Therefore, I was very careful: I always kept cash in my driver's license booklet!

Visible from the Nassau Beach Hotel was Balmoral Island, accessible only by boat. One evening, the beach rental service folks arranged a party on the island. We left after work on one of their rental boats, with some water skis, for the party on the little island. When it was time to go home, our boat wouldn't start. We had to wait until daybreak to get some help from the main island.

The morning after a "rough" night out, you ate boiled fish - a very spicy fish and potato soup in a broth with bacon, onions and red peppers. It was served with a dish of grits and a Heineken. There is nothing better for a hangover. By the way, the best way to make **Boiled Fish with Grits** is to use the fish head. When the fishing boats come in, the fish is always cheaper without the fish head because the fish head makes the best soup and is very popular with the natives.

There was no agricultural industry in the Islands. At certain times of the year, you could buy local potatoes, tomatoes, onions, sweet potatoes and peppers. Everything else had to be shipped from the United States mainland - generally out of Miami, Florida. Certain seafood items like grouper, snapper, yellow tail, conch and the clawless lobster, known as rock lobster or spiny lobster, were caught in local waters and sold immediately at the harbor. With these items and some of the local produce, the Bahamian natives had developed a very interesting and quite delicious cuisine including: **Conch Fritters**; conch chowder; **Bahamian Conch Salad**; cracked conch; Bahamian-style snapper or grouper with fried plantains and peas and rice; boiled fish and grits (which I mentioned above for a hangover); and grilled lobster tail with drawn butter. All of the dishes were quite spicy because the Bahamians loved to prepare their food with tiny hot peppers. Beef and lamb dishes were also always favorites on the menu. Iceberg and romaine lettuce were the only known salad greens for which we used four or five different salad dressings. For dessert, anything with coconut, lime or pineapple was always a hit. The beverage menu had all sorts of mixed drinks, lots of European beers, Portuguese wines called Mateus and Lancers Rose, Blue Nun Liebfraumilch and the occasional French import.

At the end of July 1963, Manfred Boll left the Nassau Beach Hotel to accept the executive chef position at the Lucayan Beach Hotel on Grand Bahama Island. At the same time, I was offered the *sous chef* position at Nassau Airport Catering. So I also left the Nassau Beach Hotel. This new position offered day-shift work, so Margot and I could spend more time together. Plus, I earned a higher salary. Furthermore, since their executive chef, Hans Schenk, was planning to return to his winter job at the Balmoral Club at the end of October, I hoped there was a possibility that I would be promoted to the executive chef position. As it turns out, things went well for me there, and I indeed became executive chef at Nassau Airport Catering on November 1, 1963.

In those days, there was a motor sports club in Nassau, and Hans Schenk was an active member of the club. Occasionally the club organized local races in which Hans participated. He drove an Austin Healey, a Jaguar E-Type and a Shelby Cobra. I was the proud owner of a Volkswagen Beetle. Somehow, Hans convinced me that I should join the club to race my 35-horsepower car. At the Volkswagen dealership, I knew some Germans, Henry von Rosenstiehl, Walter Wingenrot and Gary Wegener (the service manager), who told me that they could make my car a little more competitive with a new clutch, a second carburetor, a heavy duty camshaft and Michelin racing tires. Why not? I would race in the same class as the Mini Coopers, Mini Minors, Triumph TR3s and Triumph TR4s. These cars were water cooled, so that in a 100-mile race, they ran hot and dropped out after 70 or 80 miles. I figured that all I had to do with my little air-cooled Beetle was drive nice and steady, and I would have a chance of doing well.

"Speed Week," which was held the first week of every December and staged by the Bahamian government to promote tourism, was an exciting time. Race car drivers along with their cars came from the U.S. and Europe for the event. All week long there were all kinds of different races for all types of sports cars. A 100-mile race was specifically for Volkswagens and Formula Vee, an open-wheel, single-seater Volkswagen. I had registered to drive in this Volkswagen race. However, when I asked my manager if I could have the week off for this event, he declined. So, on the spot, I quit my job.

In the meantime, a friend of mine from the Nassau Beach Hotel had become the executive chef at the Paradise Island's Ocean Club - the only hotel on the island. He offered me the *chef garde manger,* or pantry chef, position, working daily from three in the afternoon until 11 in the evening, and I accepted. The Ocean Club was a first class hotel with 52 guest rooms, which belonged to Huntington Hartford, the heir of A&P stores and the owner of all of Paradise Island. After I communicated this job offer to the managers at Nassau Airport Catering, they suddenly changed their minds and decided to allow me to take the week off - as long as I returned to work after the vacation. Now I needed to do some quick thinking and negotiating. I didn't want to let my friend down, but at the same time I had to think about my future. I knew the Ocean Club would close in April after the season, and I needed a job for the summer of 1964. After some negotiating, we agreed that I would stay with Nassau Airport Catering with new working hours from 6am - 2pm. That way I had exactly one hour to drive from the airport to downtown, take the water taxi to Paradise Island, and start working at The Ocean Club at 3pm. So, for four months, I had two jobs and worked 18 hours every day of the week. During this time, I made more money than I could spend.

So, I got to participate in Speed Week. I finished the races in the middle of the field and lost four fenders. I was beat by Dan Gurney, A.J. Foyt and the Rodriquez brothers from Mexico.

With the Bahamas' warm weather, beautiful beaches, abundant sunshine, clear water and delicious food and beverages, everybody was happy. Even for the working people on the island, life was good. We earned decent tax-free money and there was always something going on. Almost every week someone had something to celebrate with a party that lasted until the wee morning hours. Our time in Nassau was truly unforgettable.

Boiled Snapper with Grits
Yields 6 Portions

Ingredients

For the Broiled Snapper
6-5oz Snapper Fillet
to taste Salt
to taste Freshly Ground Black Pepper
2 Tbsp Fine Chopped Parsley/Thyme/Basil
¼ tsp Fine Chopped Scotch Bonnet Peppers
1 ½ cups Sliced Onions, cut not too fine
1 cup Julienned Bacon or Salt Pork
3 cups ¼" Dice Potatoes
2 each Limes, juiced
2 oz Unsalted Butter
1 qt Water

For the Grits
3 cups Water
¾ cups White Grits
to taste Salt
4 Tbsp Unsalted Butter

Method

1. Season the snapper with salt, pepper, herbs and hot peppers. Place all of the ingredients into a large pot. Simmer for 30 minutes – the potatoes should be well cooked, but the fish should be firm.
2. Bring the water to a boil and pour in the grits.
3. Simmer for about 30 minutes. Remove from the heat and let stand with a lid on for about 10 minutes.
4. Place the cooked grits in 6 side dishes with 1 teaspoon of butter on top. The boiled snapper should be served in a separate bowl.
5. An ice-cold Heineken goes very well with this dish.

Conch Fritters
Yields about 30-34 fritters

Ingredients

1 lb Conch Meat, fine diced or run through the meat grinder with a large die
2 oz Onions, small diced
2 oz Celery, small diced
2 oz Green Bell Peppers, small diced
1 each Egg, beaten
12 oz All-purpose Flour
½ oz Baking Powder
to taste Salt
to taste Freshly Ground Pepper
to taste Tabasco
as needed Water
1 Qt Canola Oil, for deep frying

Method

1. Place the first 4 ingredients in a bowl and combine well. Reserve.
2. Mix the eggs, flour, baking powder and seasoning (salt, pepper, Tabasco) with sufficient water to form a fairly firm batter.
3. Combine the batter with the first four ingredients and let rest before deep frying.
4. Heat the canola oil to 375F. Form the conch fritters using two teaspoons to approximately 1 oz quenelles and drop in the hot oil. When golden brown, remove them from the oil and place on paper towels. Serve with a spicy remoulade.

Bahamian Conch Salad
Yields 4 Portions

Ingredients

2 cup Diced Fresh Conch
¼ cup Small Diced Celery
¼ cup Small Diced Sweet Green Bell Peppers
¼ cup Small Diced Onions
¼ cup Seeded and Diced Tomatoes
½ cup Lime Juice
to taste Hot peppers (like Habanero, Serrano, Jalapeño or similar), very fine diced
to taste Salt
to taste Freshly Ground Black Pepper

Method

1. Place all ingredients in a bowl and mix well. Let rest for at least two hours before serving.
2. In the islands, people like to eat their food very spicy. Depending on you and your guests' tastes, use the peppers accordingly.

Visitors from Germany

When we were in the water, we saw a shark circling us and Fred decided to try to catch the shark - "native style."

Since both Margot and I were working - and I had two jobs - our cash flow improved tremendously. We began to think of ways to spend the money. Since we had not seen our parents in two years, we invited them for a visit to the islands. Margot's mother was unable to travel such a long distance, but her father and my parents accepted our invitation. The plan was that they would fly to Nassau, and return to Europe by ship from New York City. We bought the tickets, rented an apartment for them and, before we knew it, welcomed them at the airport. Everyone was so excited. They were to stay in Nassau for three weeks. Then Margot and I would take a week-long vacation with them. We would all fly to Miami, stay there for two days, and then drive a rental car to New York City. Things rarely go as planned.

After just ten days, my mother had to return to Germany. The hot, muggy climate was bad for her heart condition. Unfortunately, we had failed to consider this when we booked the trip. However, our fathers stayed in the Bahamas, and had a great time. When Margot and I were at work, our friends entertained them. They experienced Bahamian life: fishing, boating and spending time on the beach. Of course, they sampled different, delicious foods and cocktails. They really made the most of their vacation.

A couple days before our departure to Miami, my friend, Fred, the pastry chef at the Nassau Beach Hotel, took us snorkeling and spear fishing in his boat. When we were in the water, we saw a shark circling us and Fred decided to try to catch the shark - "native style." He had a 30-by-30-inch plywood board with a hole in the middle, a six-foot chain and hook on one side and a 20-foot line with a buoy at the end on the other side of the board. The idea is to place a freshly caught fish on the hook, then throw the entire contraption into the water. The shark takes the bait, gets hooked and tries to swim away. Instead of floating, the board hugs the shark, drags it down and wears the poor creature out. The boaters follow the buoy. When the buoy stops moving, they throw the buoy in the boat and drag the shark onto land. It took us only about five minutes to hook the shark and another 20 minutes to land it on the beach. As we butchered the six-foot finned fish, we discovered that his stomach was empty. He had been very hungry! We gave the meat to the locals -

except for a piece of its big fin that my father insisted on keeping.

I didn't pay much attention to what my father did with that fin, until I entered his hotel room in Miami a couple days later. Something smelled absolutely awful! When I wrinkled my nose in disgust, my father confessed that he had hoped to take the fin to Germany as a souvenir. It was in his toiletry bag. Well, we did what any sensible father-son team would do: We flushed the would-be souvenir down the toilet at the Columbus Hotel in Miami.

Then it was time to begin our trip from Miami to New York City. It was a bit stressful at first since my father and I couldn't agree which road to travel. I wanted to take the fast interstate, I-95, so we could arrive in New York in just 2-1/2 days. He wanted to drive the old state road A1A along the coast to see the United States of America. He didn't realize how big the United States of America actually was. After crawling along A1A for 50 miles, wasting time and stopping at multiple fruit stands where my father bought grapefruits, oranges and tangerines, he finally saw my point. After that, we had a relatively quick journey on I-95. Late in the afternoon of the third day, we arrived in New York City.

For the next two days, we explored the city together - a great finale for their vacation. On the afternoon of the third day, they boarded the ship, *Hanseatic*, with a bag of grapefruit and a bag of oranges, to set sail for Germany. Just before they departed, they told us much how they appreciated the vacation and how very proud they were of our accomplishments.

The next day, Margot and I flew back to the Bahamas, back to work, back to our daily routine. And at this point, we started making plans for the future.

Making Plans

One day I served Dr. Martin Luther King, Jr. lunch and another day I saw The Beatles jump in the pool!

What a great week with our fathers! But now it was time for us to get back to our jobs - Margot to her liquor store and I to the catering business, making food for the airlines that flew to Nassau. In November my brother, now a chef, wrote to us that he would like to join us in the Bahamas. I found him a job at the *Nassau Beach Hotel*, where they had a new executive chef, Marcel from France - a real gentleman and a great culinarian.

Speed Week came again in December. During the past year I had become more involved with the local sports car club. Just like last year, I needed one week off for Speed Week. Just like last year, my manager denied my vacation request. Guess what? Just like last year, I quit my job and enjoyed the races for a week. But I knew I needed to find another job quickly because if the authorities discover that you are unemployed in the islands, you get deported. As the season had just begun, I figured that I would find something. I asked Marcel about employment at the Nassau Beach Hotel. He told me, "Three weeks ago I had some openings, but I hired your brother and some other staff, so I have a full culinary brigade." But then he mentioned that the hotel had just bought a new dishwasher and he maybe had an opening for a head steward - a fancy word for the head dishwasher. In that role I would train and supervise the other cleaning staff, from 7pm until midnight. Marcel also generously offered me a part-time job in the morning to take my total weekly hours to 40: I would work at the pool kitchen, cooking burgers and franks and making sandwiches. I accepted the job, even though I made $30 per month less than my brother, who had just arrived on the island. One day I served Dr. Martin Luther King, Jr. lunch and another day I saw The Beatles jump in the pool!

It was a good winter season. Margot made more money selling liquor than I did washing dishes, but that's life. Since we had already been in the Bahamas for more than two years, we thought it was time to see some more of the world. Australia would be a great place to see next. So, at the end of March, we sent our passports and paperwork to the Australian Consulate in Trinidad for the visa application. We gave notice to our employers since we were leaving at the end of April. However, before relocating to another country, we planned to get married in Germany.

At the beginning of April, though, I saw an advertisement in the *Nassau Guardian* that a private golf club in Pennsylvania was looking for a *sous chef*. I told Margot that - just for the fun of it - we should find out more about this American position. The club manager worked at a small club at Nassau's Paradise Island in the winter and at Laurel Valley Golf Club in Ligonier, Pennsylvania in the summer. So, I called to ask for an interview. We met, and he explained the position to us. Not only did he have a job for me, but he also had an office position available for Margot. Although it sounded like a very good deal, I confessed our two dilemmas that we did not have U.S. green cards and we wanted to get married. To our surprise, he told us that neither "dilemma" was a problem. We could obtain green cards in a short time, and the club did not open until the end of May, giving us plenty of time to get married.

Margot and I had a lengthy discussion about this potential change of plans. Finally, when I remarked that Pennsylvania is quite a bit closer to Germany than Australia, we decided to go to Pennsylvania. The next day we accepted the offer. We retrieved our passports from the Australian Consulate in Trinidad, and completed the necessary paperwork for our U.S. green cards. We had an interview at the U.S. Consulate, where they granted us papers to enter the U.S. as official immigrants. At the end of April, we left for Germany, got married and enjoyed one week of honeymooning. The third week of May, we moved to Ligonier, Pennsylvania.

Working in a private club was a completely new experience for me, but we'll save those details for the next chapter.

Working at a Private Club

The club's golf pro was Arnold Palmer, and President Eisenhower was an honorary member, which may have influenced the quick turnaround on our green cards.

After a wonderful three weeks in Germany, seeing our parents and old friends, getting married and traveling through Europe, we arrived in Ligonier, Pennsylvania at the end of May. The club provided us with a nice little apartment that was just a few minutes from the clubhouse where we would be working.

After unpacking, a big surprise awaited me at the clubhouse. The manager, Mr. Brandon, announced that his executive chef had decided not to show up for the season. The board and Mr. Brandon had already concluded that I would be the new executive chef! Well, I've always embraced a good challenge, and this particular challenge happened to mean more money. Of course, I accepted the offer.

The Laurel Valley Golf Club was a very special, high-end establishment with only 130 members, who were all CEOs or vice presidents from the Mellon Bank and Pittsburgh's steel industry. It was an all men's club; women were never allowed in the clubhouse. Women were permitted to play golf only on Sundays and to eat on the terrace. Male golfers are easy to please, which is not always true of female golfers, so I hoped for a rainy Sunday all summer. But - on the contrary - every Sunday was sunny that summer.

The club's golf pro was Arnold Palmer, and President Eisenhower was an honorary member, which may have influenced the quick turnaround on our green cards. The club hosted the PGA tournament in July that year. But, it was catered by an outside vendor.

For lunch, we typically served a buffet loaded with cold cuts, salads and some hot items. For dinner, we served a la carte dishes. We also provided meals for business meetings hosted by the club. Our menu consisted of typical American food of the time - like steaks, prime rib and hamburgers. In 1964, the American palate was not particularly sophisticated.

Every Monday when the club was closed, Margot and I explored the beautiful countryside around Ligonier, including Seven Springs, in our new Volkswagen station wagon. (We had purchased the car while we were in Germany and had shipped it to the U.S.) We frequently visited the local demolition derby, and enjoyed stopping at produce stands. While we usually packed a picnic of sandwiches and fruits for our outings, sometimes we stopped at a diner to sample Pennsylvania's cuisine.

At the club, Margot worked mainly in the office. However, during lunch, she served at the buffet, helping members heap food onto their plates. One particularly sunny day, President Eisenhower played golf at the club, and came into the clubhouse for lunch. Although Margot offered to serve him, he was a very uncomplicated man and he helped himself. He did not, however, use the serving utensils. He simply picked up the cold cuts from the platter with his fingers, leaving Margot quite shocked.

The summer passed quickly, and the club was to close at the end of September. In August, I received a call from a friend I had met at Nassau Beach. He had moved to Jamaica to be the general manager for the *Tryall Golf and Beach Club*, located 15 miles west of Montego Bay on Jamaica's north coast. He asked whether I was interested in being his executive chef. Winter was just around the corner, so we hopped on the chance to move to a warmer climate.

Tryall Golf and Beach Club: Jamaica

During dinner, a floor show with limbo dancers and fire eaters and the like was provided for the guests' entertainment.

A t the end of September, we packed our belongings into our Volkswagen station wagon and headed toward Miami, Florida. Since my first day of work wasn't until October 15, we spent a little time sightseeing on our way to Florida.

When we arrived in Miami, we left our car with some friends, and purchased a round-trip ticket to Montego Bay. Since my work permit hadn't come through yet, we arrived in Jamaica as "tourists." (Two of the most-used phrases in Jamaica are "soon come" and "no problem, mon," which explains a lot of the situation with my work permit status and everything else.) My friend, Ed, the general manager, picked us up at the airport and after a 15-mile drive along a bumpy road on the north shore, we arrived at Tryall.

We were immediately struck by the natural beauty of island with its lush, tropical vegetation. Bright bougainvillea and waving palm trees delighted us. We discovered that you could plant a branch or a twig from a tree or bush, and in about a week, it would start growing.

In addition to the natural beauty, we found the Jamaican people to be very friendly. Of course it took us a month or two to begin to understand their culture. We learned that things don't get done right away; Jamaicans worked at a much slower pace than we were accustomed to. It must have been the hot weather! But after we adjusted to this mentality, we began to make progress.

The Tryall Golf and Beach Club was a 6,000-acre property with a hotel, a golf course, tennis courts and many private "cottages." The cottages were actually luxury three- to five-bedroom homes complete with a maid, a cook, a gardener and a laundry lady. The club provided us with lodging - at first a hotel room and later staff quarters - and board on the property.

The club had horses for the guests - and us - to ride. The horse and guest meandered around the property for about 1-1/2 hours, and then the horses got tired and liked to run home. Once in a while they trotted right over the green on the golf course.

When my work permit finally arrived, I became an official employee at the club. I was the executive chef and the food and beverage manager. Among the club's 600 employees, there were only two foreigners - the Swiss general manager and I. As a trained chef, I was paid a pretty generous salary. The local workers lived in the mountains and walked an hour or two each way to work every day. I was shocked to learn not only how far they had to travel to work, but also how little the local people earned.

My first task was to organize the kitchen. I had some breakfast and lunch cooks and several dinner cooks, and we produced really delicious food. We had a facility on the beach where we served lunch daily and set up a Jamaican dinner buffet once or twice a week for the hotel and cottage guests. During dinner, a floor show with limbo dancers and fire eaters and the like was provided for the guests' entertainment. Somehow, it became my responsibility to find, hire and transport the entertainment. Did you know that executive chefs recruit and shuttle entertainment? That was Ed's idea; he was always thinking outside the box, so to speak.

One of Ed's crazier ideas was the pool. The clubhouse was perched on a hillside, and Ed decided to build a swimming pool - complete with a swim-up pool bar - overlooking the whole area. He designed and built the pool himself instead of hiring contractors as he wanted to employ the locals to help them earn some money. Together with our crew of Jamaicans, we dove right into the project. First we dug the hole. Then we purchased a small concrete mixer and the necessary cement and sand. And the concrete pouring commenced. We formed a long bucket line with about 40 men lined up leading from the concrete mixer to the construction site. The first man in line received a bucket full of concrete from the mixer and passed it to the next man in line and so on. The concrete passed to all 40 men before it was ultimately poured into the would-be pool. Then the empty bucket went back down the line. Now, if you've ever poured concrete, you know that once you begin, you cannot take a break. It took us seven solid days - 24 hours a day - to finish. The completed pool was gorgeous and extremely successful. It boasted spectacular views and big breezes. If you can find a good spot out of the wind, you can enjoy a very fine day of swimming, soaking and imbibing at the swim-up bar to this day.

When it comes to cuisine, Jamaica is well known for certain produce like breadfruit, a starchy tropical fruit that is used as a vegetable; *ackee*, Jamaica's national fruit that's also eaten as a vegetable, often with fish; yams, a starchy root vegetable; and mangoes. Natives cook fish with peppers on open fires on the street. Jamaicans also roast breadfruit over an open fire. Prepared this way, the breadfruit is very dry, but with lots of butter it's quite pleasant. Red peas - which are actually beans - are prepared with salt pork and green bananas, and are served as a soup. The bananas in this dish are too green to peel; the skins are cut off. ***Jamaican Meat Patties*** and ***Lobster Curry*** are also quite popular Jamaican dishes.

About once a week, we shopped for food at the local market. Fisherman, however, brought their catch directly to the hotel for us to purchase, which was very convenient. We honed our bargaining skills with them.

We lived on the north side of the island, and sometimes on Sundays we crossed the entire island to the southern coast to enjoy crayfish that were cooked with little hot red peppers. It was similar to New Orleans style crayfish, but much spicier. We drank rum and ginger ale to extinguish the fire in our mouths - or at least to numb it somewhat.

During our time in Jamaica, we made new friends, including an Italian couple, Pino and Daniela Maffesanti. Pino owned a construction business and built "cottages" at Tryall - mostly for the Americans. When they finished the roof on a new cottage, the new homeowner paid for a topping-off party with a delicious goat water "soup" made with goat, yams, bananas and all kinds of vegetables. The beverages consumed at these festivities were 151-proof rum with a homemade ginger ale and the locally-made Red Stripe beer. The goat water was prepared by the construction crew's wives and girlfriends. After 40 years, the Maffesantis are still our friends. We visit each other in Jamaica and Italy.

We also met a couple from Chicago, Jack and Dorothy Harrison, who became almost like second parents to us. When we discovered that Margot was pregnant with our first child, Kirsten, the Harrisons invited Margot to Chicago two weeks prior to her due date, so we could have an American baby. Years later when Margot was pregnant with Susi, we were living in Germany, and Pino and Daniela were expecting in Jamaica. The Harrisons invited all four of us to Chicago for the births. Pino's daughter was born just two days after our Susi. Margot and Daniela even shared a hospital room.

But as wonderful as life was for us on the beautiful island, it became very difficult to obtain a new work permit. Therefore, we decided to leave in the fall. It was time to look for our next adventure.

Jamaican Beef Patties
Yields about 20 patties

Ingredients

For the Pastry Dough:
4 cups All Purpose Flour
2 tsp Ground Turmeric
1 tsp Table Salt
8 oz Butter, room temperature
3 Tbsp Ice Cold Water

For the Beef Filling:
2 Tbsp Butter
1 cup Yellow Onion, fine diced
2 each Large Garlic Cloves, grated with a microfile
2 each Habanero Peppers, seeded and fine chopped
1 tsp Fresh Thyme, fine chopped
2 Tbsp Chives, short cut
2 Tbsp Italian Parsley, fine chopped
3 cups Diced Fresh Tomatoes
12 oz 80/20 Ground Beef
¼ tsp Ground Turmeric
½ tsp Grated Fresh Ginger
¼ tsp Ground Cumin
1 tsp Jamaican Allspice
½ tsp Ground Cardamom
to taste Salt
to taste Black Pepper
½ cup Beef Stock
2 Tbsp Jamaican Brown Rum

Jamaican Beef Patties

Method

1. In a bowl, mix the flour, turmeric and salt together.
2. Add the butter and mix with your fingers until it resembles breadcrumbs.
3. Add the water (3 Tbsp or more) to form a dough.
4. Wrap the dough in plastic wrap and place in a refrigerator for several hours before using.
5. Put the butter in a large sauce pan and add the onions, garlic, hot peppers, thyme, chives, parsley and tomatoes; sauté until soft.
6. Add the rest of the ingredients except the rum. Cook everything over medium heat until all of the liquid is evaporated and the mixture is really thick.
7. Add the rum to the mixture and remove the pot from the fire. Let the mixture cool.
8. Preheat the oven to 400° F.
9. To put the patties together, roll out the pastry dough and cut with 10" fluted round cutters. On one side of the rounds, put 1 ½ Tbsp of beef filling. Brush the edges of the side the beef filling is on with egg wash. Fold the empty side over so the edges meet and crimp down with a fork. Make sure that the edges are well sealed.
10. Place the patties on a sheet pan covered with a Silpat, brush with egg wash and put into the preheated oven. Bake for about 30 minutes until golden brown.

Lobster Curry
Yields 5 Portions

Ingredients

4 Tbsp Canola Oil
1 tsp Cumin Seeds
3 each Garlic Cloves, minced
½ each Jalapeno Pepper, finely diced
1½ Tbsp Masala Curry for seafood or Regular Curry
2 Tbsp All-purpose Flour
1 tsp Fine Chopped Parsley
1 tsp Short-cut Chives
1 tsp Chopped Fresh Thyme
1½ cups Peeled, Seeded and Diced Roma Tomatoes or 1 small can diced tomatoes
2-3 cups Water
to taste Salt
to taste Freshly Ground Black Pepper
1lb Cooked Lobster Meat (languste)

Method

1. Place the canola oil in a sauce pot and add the cumin seeds, garlic and jalapeno pepper. Sauté everything until the garlic almost turns a little brown.
2. Add the curry and flour. Stir until it forms a smooth paste.
3. Add the herbs and tomatoes. Mix well.
4. Add the water and create a sauce. Bring the sauce to a boil and then simmer for 10 minutes.
5. Season to taste with salt and pepper.
6. Add the lobster meat, reheat and serve with rice.

French Leave Hotel on Eleuthera Island/Bahamas

*The family he worked for owned a fantastic winter home in Nassau called Rock
Point that was once featured in the James Bond movie, Thunderball.*

Our next adventure took us back to the Bahamas, at the French Leave Hotel
on the Island of Eleuthera. The French Leave was a 45-room hotel on a
gorgeous, 7-mile pink sand beach. The hotel was privately-owned by an
American actor, who stayed on Eleuthera in the winter and spent summers
in Rome. The hotel operated from November until July or August, and then
it closed for three months. I was the executive chef and the kitchen staff was mostly
from Eleuthera except one young man from England.

The entire facility only had one fresh-water tap. All of the guest rooms were
supplied with salt water for showering and tooth brushing. Boats from Miami
delivered gallons of fresh water every week that we distributed to our guests; each
room received one gallon a day.

Hotel management provided us with living quarters, a house supplied with salt
water located about a half mile from the hotel. Every day I carried two five-gallon
containers of water home from the hotel for our personal washing and laundry.
Kirsten was just an infant, and was happy in her mosquito-net-covered crib.

After being there for six months, our friend, Hans, a chauffeur we had met in
Nassau years earlier, contacted us. The family he worked for owned a fantastic
winter home in Nassau called Rock Point that was once featured in the James Bond
movie, *Thunderball*. The home had two pools - one saltwater pool and one
freshwater. They also owned a five-bedroom cottage about three miles from the
hotel. Hans informed us that the family was looking for someone to house sit at the
five-bedroom cottage, since they only spent two weeks a year there.

We jumped at the offer, and were thrilled to discover that the house was right on
the beach with a wonderful deck. The house was very isolated with the nearest
neighbor being a half mile away. We had several bedrooms, a living room, a kitchen
and about two acres of land. Additionally we had the use of their Pontiac, $200 a
month house-sitting income and a gardener who cared for the lawn. The
landscaping was packed with pretty poinsettias - in every color. I started a vegetable
garden, and planted everything in straight rows. The gardener sprinkled some

watermelon seeds all over the property, and all of the sudden we had 130 ripe watermelons!

We also grew bananas there. We discovered that you could replant a banana shoot and after nine months you had a mature plant with a huge stem of bananas. I had never seen a banana plant growing before, and was amazed to learn that bananas grow on a long stem in tiers, or hands, with about 20 bananas to a hand and as many as 5 or more hands on one stem. Really prolific plants may contain as many as 20 hands, for a single harvest of 400 bananas. And to complicate things, when one banana ripens, within a day or two so do all the rest. We had bananas coming out of our ears. We ate bananas for breakfast, lunch and dinner. **Bananas Foster** was always fun. Plus we sipped delicious banana daiquiris later in the evenings.

When the hotel closed for the season, they kept me on payroll. In the off season, I only had to cook for seven people - the accountant, the secretary, the housekeeper, the general manager and his wife and the assistant manager and his wife. I had one woman who helped in the kitchen, and I trained her to prepare breakfast and lunch, so I only had to cook dinner. Breakfast was at 8am sharp; lunch was at noon; and dinner was at 6pm. If you weren't there - too bad - you missed it.

We cooked numerous seafood dishes using lobster, snapper, grouper and yellow tail. The best local product was the lobster/*langusta*. When the price was right, I would buy a whole boatload of lobster - about 1500 pounds. Then I cooked it all, and froze the tails for the winter. Our customers really enjoyed eating Lobster Salad or **Lobster Louie**. All of the meat and vegetables came weekly by boat from Miami, as the hotel guests consumed more than you could buy locally.

Although Governor's Harbor was just a tiny village on the island, it had an airport served by Pan American Airlines. Once in a while we flew to Nassau to get back to the civilized world. Also, once a year, Margot and Kirsten went to Germany to visit for several weeks. While they were away, I spent some time on the beach and enjoyed deep-sea fishing.

In 1968, when the Bahamas became independent, it became difficult to get a work permit. The money we earned there was completely tax free, but it was, again, time to move on.

Bananas Foster
Yields 6 Portions

Ingredients

3 each Bananas, peeled and cut in half lengthwise
1 oz Unsalted Butter
1 oz Unsalted Butter
3 oz Brown Sugar
1 each Fresh Lime Juice
2 each Fresh Orange Juice
1 each Orange, zested
1 cup Orange-flavored Liquor
6 each Scoops of Vanilla Ice Cream
1 cup Whipped Cream

Method

1. Sauté the bananas with 1 oz of butter until lightly brown. Remove the bananas from the flambé pan and reserve.
2. Add 1 oz of butter and the brown sugar. Sauté until the sugar is melted.
3. Add lime juice, orange juice and orange zest and cook for 2-3 minutes.
4. Return the bananas to the flambé pan and add the liquor. Flambé.
5. Place a half banana on each of the 6 plates. Nape the bananas with the cooking liquid. Put 1 scoop of vanilla ice cream on each plate. Garnish with a dollop of whipped cream. Serve immediately.

Lobster Louie
Yields 4 Portions

Ingredients

¾ cup Mayonnaise
¼ cup Fine Diced Celery
¼ cup Fine Diced Red Bell Peppers
1 Tbsp Fine Diced Onion
1 Tbsp Chopped Parsley
1 pinch Cayenne Pepper
to taste Salt
to taste Freshly Ground Black Pepper
¾ lb Lobster Meat, cooked and cut into ¼" pieces
4 each Large Lettuce Leaves
8 each Tomato Wedges

Method

1. Whisk together the first seven items to make the dressing for the salad.
2. Fold the lobster meat into the dressing and season to taste as needed with salt and pepper.
3. Place one lettuce leave on each of the four chilled plates.
4. Spoon an equal amount of lobster salad on each plate. Garnish with 2 tomato wedges per plate.

Holiday Inn at Mamora Bay and Holiday Day Inn in Barbados

There wasn't enough locally-sourced food to feed all of our guests, so once a week we flew in a truckload of groceries, including all of the necessary meat and seafood, from New York City.

A s I mentioned before, I often found out about jobs from purveyors. A New York City meat purveyor informed me of the opening that landed me an executive chef position at the new Holiday Inn on Antigua. It was a franchise operation, and the owners came from Kitchener, Ontario, Canada. They also had franchise rights to open hotels in Trinidad, Granada, St. Lucia and Barbados. The 100-room hotel was situated on a peninsula on Mamora Bay about 20 miles from St. John's, Antigua's capitol. The hotel had a casino that was privately-operated by a group of Americans from East Orange, New Jersey. It was the only casino on the island, and was very good for our hotel business.

Gambling junkets of approximately 120 people arrived on Wednesdays or Thursdays and left on Sundays. There were two kinds of junkets. First, there were the *sunshine junkets* which consisted of couples. This was not the favored group for casino management as *sunshine junkets* went to bed early and were on the beach by 7am. Second, there were the *regular junkets* that consisted of men only. The casino management really liked these groups because they gambled until four or five in the morning.

There wasn't enough locally-sourced food to feed all of our guests, so once a week we flew in a truckload of groceries, including all of the necessary meat and seafood, from New York City. I had to plan ahead to ensure we didn't run out of anything. The island had onions, tomatoes, potatoes and simple staples, but if we ran out of grapes, berries, lettuce, parsley or carrots, we were in trouble. I became pretty skilled at estimating.

We lived right on the beach in housing provided by the hotel. It was not a house like we had in Jamaica, but rather a trailer home with two bedrooms, a living room and a kitchen. We didn't own any furniture and the trailer was modestly furnished. It was nothing special, but it was free and we were comfortable there.

Since Kirsten was now about two years old, we enrolled her in preschool. Each morning the hotel's driver picked her up to take her downtown in his Jeep, and he brought her home in time for lunch. One day Kirsten wasn't home yet at noon. At 1pm, she still wasn't home and Margot began to panic. She asked the manager's wife if she knew what had happened. She did not. Around 2pm, the Jeep finally pulled up. The driver had a girlfriend in town, and he had stopped to visit her while Kirsten waited in the car! From then on Kirsten never returned to preschool.

But that didn't keep her out of trouble. When she was about three, Kirsten really enjoyed the *Curious George* books. In one book, the little monkey had swallowed something and was amazed to see it on an x-ray machine at the hospital. She asked us to read it to her over and over. One day Margot noticed that part of the barrel bolt safety slide lock on the bathroom door was missing. She asked Kirsten whether she knew where the little metal bit was. Kirsten nodded and said, "Yes, it's in my tummy." We headed to the hospital and the x-ray confirmed that she was telling the truth. Monkey see, monkey do! The doctors offered to surgically remove the lock part or we could allow it to naturally expel. We looked around the hospital where glassless windows allowed goats and chickens access to wander the hallways, and we were convinced that the natural way was best. Poor Margot had her work cut out for her for the next few days, but the problem eventually resolved itself.

We also had a problem at the hotel. About six weeks after the hotel opened, we lost power every night at 6pm - no lights, no air conditioning, nothing. The hotel was hot and dark. Maurice, an American engineer originally from Florida, who worked for the construction company that had built the hotel, maintained the two big Caterpillar generators that the hotel had purchased to provide power during blackouts. Eventually the electricity problem was resolved. On top of that, Maurice and I became great friends, and enjoyed spearfishing together.

Pan American Airlines hosted an annual spearfishing tournament. It started at 8am and went until 4pm. Prizes were given to the team who caught the most fish as well as the team that caught the largest fish. There were five people in each boat. Four team members were in the water spearfishing; the "basket man" remained in the boat and stayed close to the spearfishers to haul the fish into the boat. We were in the water for the entire eight-hour tournament, and had to wear t-shirts to avoid getting sunburned. This particular year, we caught an 85-pound stingray and were certain we had won. Unfortunately a team from St. Maarten caught a 175-pound nurse shark and defeated us.

We had good contacts at Antigua's Pan American naval base, which served as a tracking station for space expeditions. The chief security officer there, a German named Alfred von Levern, and his wife became our good friends.

Around this time, the company opened a Holiday Inn in Barbados and my brother was the executive chef there. He really didn't like it and left after just six months. Since business was slow in Antigua during the summer months, the company decided to send the other Handke - me - to Barbados. I agreed to go for no longer than six weeks. Margot and Kirsten tagged along.

Summer season in Barbados was not too bad. It was reasonably priced and packed with New Yorkers. Every week we hosted two barbecue evenings and cooked a lot of well-done steaks. After the agreed upon six short weeks, we returned to Antigua.

In Antigua, however, the political scene had changed. It had become independent in 1969 and a new party came into power. It was no longer safe to go to town. Holiday Inn management decided that the supervisory staff had to protect the hotel in case of trouble. Because the hotel was on a little peninsula, it was only approachable by the 500-yard long connection to the main island. It was very difficult to approach by sea. We didn't have guns, but the hotel planned to furnish them. When I told Margot that I might have to sit on the roof with a gun to protect the hotel, she was not at all excited about it. Our friend Maurice, who owned a power boat, offered to pick us up with his boat in case of trouble and take us to the Pan Am navy base. As it turned out, we thankfully never had to enact that plan.

Around that time, we received a letter from my father, informing us of an opportunity to take over a restaurant close to my hometown in Germany. We gave notice and left Antigua at the end of August.

Berggasthof-Hoherodskopf near Schotten, Germany

On our first camping trip, which took place before we moved to Germany, we drove from Chicago to Banff, Canada in a Volkswagen camper with a tent.

The Berggasthof-Hoherodskopf is a clubhouse that belongs to a local hiking club. In 1970, the person leasing the place was retiring. My father encouraged us to apply, so I interviewed with the board and told them my proposal to run the venue. The clubhouse had 300 seats in the restaurant, 120 seats in the summer on the terrace, 16 guest rooms and a gift shop. (Later, we added a ski, boot and sled rental service.) I was accepted and we took over in October 1970.

Located 770 meters above sea level, the Berggasthof-Hoherodskopf is a hiking destination and the only building in a three-mile radius. The facility is just 12 kilometers from Schotten, where I grew up. I remember hiking that mountain during my school years. The hike begins at 250 meters above sea level, and the eight-mile trek ascends 500 meters. In the winter we had to carry our skis up the mountain on our shoulders because there was no ski lift. We skied a small section near the top - about a mile - and then hiked back up with our skis. We would spend the whole day doing this.

On Sundays, some people flocked to the area to hike in the woods while others took leisurely walks with their dogs. Then they came to the restaurant for lunch or coffee and cake. They brought their dogs into the restaurant with them. Sometimes the dogs didn't get along and started barking. So, we had to make a rule that poorly-behaved dogs had to wait outside.

During the winter months, the parking lots were always full. Sometimes patrons had to park along the street. On holidays, there were cars parked all the way to the next village. On snowy winter school days, school buses filled with children came from surrounding cities like Frankfurt, Offenbach and Giessen. Some days we might have as many as 40 or 50 buses. Since the school children paid individually with Deutsche mark bills, before they came, we had make sure we had a lot of change - like 2000 Deutsche marks. The change was always gone by 1pm when the children left.

Margot and I were just 30 years old and very energetic. We opened each day at

7:30am for breakfast, but our primary business was lunch and afternoon coffee and cake. For lunch we served comfort food like *Schweinebraten*, or pork roast, with potato dumplings and red cabbage; *Wiener schnitzel* with French fries (which were "new" at that time); bratwurst with sauerkraut; split pea soup with vegetables and knackwurst; and a hiker's sausage plate with locally-made liver sausage, blood sausage and some other sausages. We served this dish on a wooden board with thickly-sliced sausage and bread along with pickles, cheese and tomatoes. We also served the local favorite, *Strammer Max*, which is a ham steak with a fried egg on top.

For the afternoon coffee, we had all sorts of cakes and pastries. For the first two years, I had a pastry chef, but he received an offer for a chef position and left. For the next two years, I baked all the desserts. For Sundays alone I made 10 two-foot **Apple Strudels**, eight cheesecakes, eight Black Forest cakes, plum cakes, several kinds of coffee cakes and eight sponge cakes that we served with a variety of fruits and other pastries. On Sundays we served between 1500 and 2000 pieces of cake with coffee. Naturally beer, wine and soft drinks were also consumed. To my great delight, the pastry chef returned after two years!

In the 1970s strawberries were only available during strawberry season from around the end May until the middle of June. During the strawberry season, we served strawberry torte with a glazed top and whipped cream. We made 60 tortes every Sunday. Margot's friends, Edith and Renate, from Baden-Baden, came to help with putting the strawberries on the sponge cakes on Sunday mornings. I made them whistle while they worked, so they could not eat the berries.

Another seasonal favorite in Germany is white asparagus. Only available in the spring, white asparagus is so popular that restaurants offer special *Spargelzeit*, or asparagus season, menus. We served asparagus with butter, asparagus with ham, asparagus with hollandaise sauce and - my personal favorite - **White Asparagus Soup**.

Including the pastry chef, we had nine full-time employees. In the kitchen, I worked with two chef's apprentices and one Yugoslavian immigrant woman with a work permit. We also had a handyman, three full-time servers, another Yugoslavian immigrant who cleaned the guest rooms and a woman who tended the gift shop.

On Sundays, we employed about a dozen more servers, who were teenagers between 14 and 16 years old. Because they didn't drive, I had to pick them up for work. I drove a Volkswagen bus for an entire hour to collect all of them from surrounding villages. In the evening around 6pm, I drove them all home again.

I began training culinary apprentices during this time. Some afternoons when we had bad weather, there was nothing to do because the restaurant was empty. But I tried to keep the apprentices busy. If an apprentice annoyed or upset me, I gave him some "special" tasks. One particular young man angered me almost daily. We'll call him Al. It was early December, and I said, "Al, today we are going to dry sauerkraut." Well, we strung butcher twine between two tall posts in the kitchen, and I told him to hang up sauerkraut - strand by strand - to dry it for the winter. He used little tongs that looked like tweezers to complete this project. A salesman happened to stop by and asked what Al was doing. I explained that sauerkraut must be dried for the winter. *Wink, wink.*

Another day I sent Al to a restaurant four kilometers away to pick up a *caraway seed splitting machine.* It took him about an hour to walk there through the mountainous landscape. When he arrived, the owner, whom I had phoned in advance, handed him a package containing something that weighed 30 or 40 pounds. He lugged it back to the Berggasthof. After I opened it, I informed him that he had the wrong machine. He then had to lug it all the way back to my friend. Poor fellow.

In Germany many restaurants have contracts with a local brewery. We took over the contract from a nearby brewery, and the last Saturday of October, we had a *Frei Bier Abend,* or free beer evening. A lot of hiking club members came. When they drank, they ate. There was music and singing, and it was a very nice evening. They went home around 2am or later. We never ran out of beer.

Margot and I had been married almost 10 years and we were very happy owning our own business. We lived in the clubhouse in an apartment on the second floor. We celebrated the birth of our second daughter, Susi. But we suffered one big problem: our dependence on weather.

When the weather was good - sunny summer days or snowy winter days - business was booming. During bad weather, we had no business. Because of the elevation, the weather could stall over the mountain for months. Sometimes the weather would turn to rain and fog in September and last until Christmas. When the oil crisis arrived in 1974, no one was allowed to drive in Germany on Sundays. Then, nobody came.

During our seven-year tenure there, we had only one really good winter with lots of business: 1970-1971. We learned to save our summer earnings to pay the bills in the winter. We kept the staff employed year-round, just in case business picked up. We had to make sure they didn't take jobs somewhere else.

Every four years (1972 and 1976), the Culinary Olympics and its accompanying trade show took place in Frankfurt. I worked for a restaurant equipment company at these shows, demonstrating and selling Phillips-brand microwave ovens. I showed attendees that you can put a cold cup of soup in the microwave and, in just 60 seconds, it's piping hot. It really works with the consommé - no need to even stir! Rice was a very good demonstration medium as well. One rule that I followed was: never microwave Knackwurst or wieners. They exploded and it made a bad impression.

* * *

Because business was slow, we closed every year for three weeks in November and flew to the United States. We usually started with a visit to the Harrisons in Chicago. The Harrisons had two daughters, who had attended the University of Wisconsin in Madison. Every year the Harrisons rented a motor home and invited four other couples and us to join them. We all drove from Chicago to Madison to a football game. I vividly recall the food and drinks on these trips. On the way there, we sat in the back of the motor home, playing cards and drinking Harvey Wallbangers. Then we tailgated with potato salad, bratwursts and Bloody Marys. At one particularly chilly game, I recall Mrs. Harrison brought a bottle of Cherry Heering, a Danish liqueur, to keep us warm. After the game, we enjoyed dinner in a steakhouse. We had ten people in our party, and the large table had a Lazy Susan with all kinds of pickled foods like anchovies and olives. We drank martinis. The restaurant specialized in prime rib, offering a queen's cut and a king's cut (one whole bone about 1-1/2 inches thick). The portion was so enormous that I couldn't finish it! After dinner, we stayed in a hotel. The next morning we took off and stopped in a state park to feast on scrambled eggs, bacon and hash browns that we washed down with Black Velvet, a mix of stout and champagne. Then we headed back to Chicago.

On that trip I had the opportunity to drive a motor home for the first time. I was the king of the road with 32 feet of bus behind me. What fun! As we drew closer to Chicago, we passed through an occasional traffic light. At one point, I saw a green light ahead and when I was about 50 yards away, it changed to yellow and then red. I had to make a quick decision: to hit the brakes or go through. I decided to brake, and I hit them so hard that all the Harvey Wallbangers and Bloody Marys and people flew to the front. Immediately afterwards, I was released from my driving duties.

But driving that motor home was such fun that in the following years, we rented motor homes and toured America. On our first camping trip, which took place before we moved to Germany, we drove from Chicago to Banff, Canada in a Volkswagen camper with a tent. On Highway 1, we saw 1,500 kilometers of wheat fields and silos, and were completely awed by the gleaming Lake Louise and the surrounding Canadian Rockies in Banff. I enjoyed cooking over the campfire, and recall preparing fresh trout. It was so cold that we nearly froze the first night.

Running a restaurant leaves very little time for the children, so these trips were very special - spending time close together in a motor home. We traveled to Mexico, where we had to hang our laundry on top of our motor home so it wouldn't be stolen. We saw Florida and the West Coast and many places in between. In New Orleans, Kirsten inquired about the scantily-clad women in the windows. After that, we stayed away from Bourbon Street.

* * *

Overall, the seven and a half years in Germany were great. My parents were only about six miles away. Margot's parents were just a two-hour drive on the Autobahn. We made new friends and we had clientele who were very good to us.

But being away from Germany for so long and being accustomed to living the U.S. and the islands, we had a completely different mindset. Plus Margot was from southern Germany, so she was almost like a foreigner in the north. We were called the "Americans." We didn't always feel too welcome. We were just the restaurant proprietors. At times it didn't really feel like home anymore - especially after my mother passed away from a heart condition in 1974.

Our final winter season (1977) was a disaster. We had to think hard about what to do next. The Harrisons were encouraging us to return to the States and we still had valid green cards. So, in October 1977, we stored some of our furniture at a friend's place and sold the rest. We arrived in Chicago with six or seven suitcases on a Friday and the kids started school on Monday.

Kirsten was in 4th grade; Susi was in preschool. Susi didn't speak any English at all. Kirsten spoke a little English. Susi was stubborn and she argued with the other children when they couldn't understand each other. When I picked Susi up from school one day, the teachers told me she had misbehaved. After that, I told Margot that she would have to pick Susi up.

In November, I went to the Hotel and Motel Show in New York, and that's the way the Athletic Club came about.

Apple Strudel
Yields 6 Portions

Ingredients

1½-2 lb Apples, Macintosh or similar
2 oz All-purpose Flour
1 each Sheet of Puff Pastry (Pepperidge Farms is easy to find in the freeze aisle)
3 oz Sweet Crumbs, made from cinnamon crackers run in a food processor
5 Tbsp Sugar
1 tsp Cinnamon
4 oz Raisins
1 each Egg

Method

1. Peel the apples and then cut them in 8 wedges. Remove the core and slice them by hand or with an attachment on the food processor.
2. Sprinkle a little flour on the surface of the table as well as on the unfolded puff pastry dough. Roll out the dough a little more than the length of a half-size sheet pan and ¾s of the width of a half-size sheet pan.
3. Make a bed of sweet crumbs in the middle of the puff pastry sheet, going down the center lengthwise. Pile the sliced apples on top of the sweet crumbs. Mix the sugar and cinnamon together; sprinkle the top of the apples with the sugar/cinnamon and raisins.
4. Break the egg in a bowl and add a little water to make an egg wash. Egg wash the short ends and one side of the dough. Fold the dough side without the egg wash over the apples. Then fold the egg-washed dough side on top of it. Fold over the short ends and seal. Egg wash the whole strudel. With a paring knife make two air holes in the top of the strudel. Put the strudel into a 350F preheated oven and bake for 30-35 minutes until golden brown.

White Asparagus Soup
Yields 10 Portions

Ingredients

1 cup Unsalted Butter
1 cup All-purpose Flour
½ cup Diced Onions
2 ½-3 qt White Stock (chicken or veal)
4 cups White Asparagus peel and trimmings
1 pinch Nutmeg
to taste Salt
to taste Freshly Ground White Pepper
2 each Egg Yolks
½ cup Heavy Cream
2 cups Short cut and Cooked Asparagus Pieces

Method

1. Melt the butter and and sauté the onions until translucent.
2. Add the flour and make a roux.
3. Add the white stock and bring the mixture to a boil, stirring occasionally with a wire whisk to prevent burning on the bottom of the pot.
4. Add the asparagus peel and trimmings, simmer for at least 30 minutes.
5. Strain through a cheesecloth or chinoise.
6. Combine the egg yolks and heavy cream and fold into the hot, but not boiling, soup.
7. Add the asparagus pieces and serve.

Athletic Club of Columbus

We had never been to a Wendy's before. When we ordered hamburgers, we were shocked to see square patties.

We stayed with the Harrisons in Chicago while I searched for a job. Headhunters were not used at this time, so it was entirely up to me to find an employer. I traveled to New York for the International Hotel and Motel Show, which was a great place to make connections and talk to purveyors. I walked the show for three days, hoping to find a job with a hotel, restaurant or club. I talked to two American Culinary Federation (ACF) representatives, who were promoting their apprenticeship program that piloted in Pittsburgh. One of the gentlemen was the ACF director, Ed Brown, and the other was a Columbus, Ohio chef, Max Behr. Chef Behr asked me for my resume.

On Monday following the show, I received a call from the general manager, Hans Rawe, of the Athletic Club of Columbus (Ohio). He invited me to Columbus for an interview. I flew to Ohio the very next day, and interviewed behind locked doors. A couple days later, I accepted his job offer.

During our six-week stay with the Harrisons, Mr. Harrison invited me many times to join his men's group for their three-martini luncheons. We enjoyed several dinners at Medina Country Club, where Mr. Harrison was a member and later the president. We also bought a brand-new car - a brown Buick LaSabre. I told the salesman I would pay for the car with $6500 cash. When I asked about a cash discount, I learned quickly that discount-for-cash programs didn't exist in the U.S. Our Buick was a big, comfortable car with a bench seat across the front. A few days later, we packed the car and started driving.

We planned to drive Interstate 65 south to Indianapolis, and then go east on I-70 to Columbus. Just 30 miles out of Chicago, however, the interstate was closed because of drifting snow. We stopped at a smoky, packed Stuckey's Restaurant, where everyone was stranded. A highway patrolman informed us that the road would not re-open that day. He suggested that we drive back north to the turnpike, drive east to Toledo and then travel south on Route 23. So we started out again.

The road was treacherous with snow and ice. We saw so many accidents - cars overturned and semi-trucks in the ditches. We finally arrived at the Athletic Club at

1am. People were pouring out of the building with big bags, and I said to Margot, "It looks like we missed the Christmas party!"

My new boss, Mr. Rawe, had advised me in advance to check in as guests when we arrived at the club. The current chef, who was preparing for a large party at the club on Saturday, didn't know I had been hired. Mr. Rawe was afraid that, if this chef found out about me, he might walk out before Saturday's party.

Saturday morning was very quiet in the club. Mr. Rawe came in late, and met with me on the third floor. We had already agreed on my $21,000 salary. He told me that my first day of work was Monday morning. We were free the rest of the weekend. So on Saturday evening, we acquired our first impressions of Columbus.

Near the club was the first-ever Wendy's restaurant. We had never been to a Wendy's before. When we ordered hamburgers, we were shocked to see square patties. I asked Margot, "What's this?!?" I declared right then and there, "No more Wendy's for me!" Subsequently, I did not dine at another Wendy's again until the 1990s when I was on a site inspection trip in Lancaster, Ohio with a couple of my employees. I had seen a television commercial with Dave Thomas advertising his new, delicious-looking bacon and onion hamburger, so I decided to give Wendy's a second chance. That bacon-topped burger was damn good!

On our first weekend in Columbus, we tried very hard to blend in as well-mannered guests at the club. Sunday evening, after a Chinese dinner, the receptionist at the club started making some small talk with us. Susi, a fairly typical three-and-a-half-year old, took off running. She ran to the elevator, hit the button, hopped into the lift and was gone! The Athletic Club has two elevators and a lovely swimming pool on the fifth floor. Susi's elevator climbed to the fifth floor and stopped. So we rushed into the second elevator to rescue her from the potential dangers of the pool. We arrived on the fifth floor just as the doors of her elevator were closing. Now Susi's elevator was heading down. So we pushed the lobby button. This continued for several trips up and down before we were finally timed it just right to grab Susi. So much for being inconspicuous guests that weekend at an exclusive club.

In 1977, the Athletic Club was the second best club in town. The Columbus Club was number one, while the University Club also gave the Athletic Club a run for their money. At this time, the Athletic Club of Columbus was exclusively a men's club. Women were only permitted entrance as guests of their husbands, and they were only allowed to eat in one dining room, the Crystal Room on the second floor. Women were never permitted in The Stag Bar. The club had an athletic director and boasted state-of-the-art facilities, including a squash court, an Olympic-sized swimming pool, a bowling alley and other recreational opportunities. Membership was not cheap.

For the members, the club was more or less their second home. Some members came every day for lunch, and every day they ordered the same food. One member insisted on cottage cheese with canned fruit cocktail. Another member always ordered a hamburger. Every Friday we offered the same two chowders - one clear (Manhattan) and one creamy (New England). Those chowders, and all of the other soups, needed a bit of attention when I first arrived. The members were accustomed to - really quite attached to - the club's thick soups. The spoon had to stand up in the soup! After a difficult first six months, I was finally able to convert them to my way of thinking and cooking. But the soup was not the only item on the menu in need of some adjustment.

One morning during my first six months at the club, Mr. Rawe, over coffee, introduced me to the club's president. The president said, "Young man, let me tell you something. My grandmother bakes a better apple pie than what you serve our members here!" As you can imagine, this comment bothered me. I made it my goal to do something about it.

Our members ordered so few desserts that it did not make sense to bake fresh pies. So, we bought delicious apple pies from one of our purveyors, and kept them in the cooler. But, at that time, it was customary to serve warm apple pie with a slice of cheddar cheese melted on top. To do this, we took the apple pie out of the cooler every day and placed it above the range to warm it. When an order came in, we placed a slice of cheese on a piece of pie and placed it under the broiler. Letting the pie sit out all day proved to be the trouble. To solve this problem, I suggested we purchase a microwave oven, so the apple pie could stay fresh in the cooler. The next day we had a microwave in the kitchen! Now we could take one slice of pie at a time from the cooler when needed.

In addition to the microwave, I requested some other equipment, including a new grill. The old grill was heated from the top - like a broiler. The new grill only heated from the bottom - like a charcoal grill. On the new grill, the hamburgers tasted more like charcoal, and the members didn't like them anymore! It took a full six months for them to get used to the new flavor.

December is not a good time to take over a club kitchen operation because it is the busiest time of the year. Every day for lunch we had 10-16 parties. Mr. Rawe's assistant and secretary, Carol Howard, managed sales for these parties and created all the menus. She was wonderful. She had no problem selling different vegetables and different starches to each party, so that we had to prepare 16 vegetables and 16 starches on the same day. I gently and firmly told her this practice had to stop. "If we have cauliflower today," I said, "then EVERYBODY gets cauliflower." I explained to her that the club had lost money last year in food operations, and that I planned to remedy that. When I saw she was close to tears, I added, "Well maybe you can offer two different vegetables, but that's it." Yes, that was a very challenging month. Because I wasn't accustomed to the American way of celebrating the holidays, I really had to scramble.

The club had a policy - typical of most clubs at this time - requiring each member to spend a minimum of $50 per month on food. Nevertheless, the year before I arrived, the club had lost $120,000 in the food operations. After the first year I was there, however, I improved this to a $65,000 profit. This financial turnaround also benefitted my wallet. My bonus agreement was: if my food cost did not exceed 32% per month, then I received a $100 bonus. If I my kitchen labor cost did not exceed 12%, I received an additional $100 bonus. In the eight and a half years that I worked there, I never lost those bonuses. Mr. Rawe was a very good manager who really knew the business - both the numbers and the food. Plus he was German, so we hit it off really well.

In the meantime, Margot and the girls were getting used to living in Columbus. After staying at the club for the first week, we then rented a flimsy house in nearby Upper Arlington. It was very stressful working and getting everything organized for my family, since we needed so much, including furniture. That year we bought our Christmas tree at a place on Morse Road. It was the ugliest tree we ever had, but we put real German candles on the tree, so it felt a little bit like home. On January 26, 1978, we woke up at 6am to a big blizzard. Margot told me I could not go to work. So, I called Mr. Rawe, who confirmed I should stay home. As it turns out, our family arrived in Ohio just in time to experience the Great Blizzard of 1978! The next day, however, I made it to work, along with a handful of staff who lived nearby.

After about six months, we decided to buy a house. In Germany, you pay for your new home with cash. Were we ever thrilled to learn about mortgages! We bought a nice house in Upper Arlington with a two-car garage. Then, I surprised Margot with a Volkswagen Golf. The dealership delivered it to our house, and I got up early to put a ribbon on the new car. At breakfast I gave Margot a miniature VW Golf, and she said, "What should I do with this?" Then she discovered the car outside. For the first time we were a two-car family.

Margot and I originally planned to stay at the club for only two years because after that we wanted to own a restaurant. But after two years, I was king of the club. Everyone loved my food. I remember Mr. Rawe calling me to his office to congratulate me on a successful year. Every year he increased my salary two or three times. I never had to ask for a raise. Then he told me the club was doing away with the food minimum because my food was drawing a crowd. I figured that was a good time to make a request.

The club granted me three weeks of paid vacation per year, so I asked whether I could have four weeks. We always took one week of vacation in the spring. Then in August the club was closed for two weeks. I proposed to leave two weeks before the club closed, and then return three days before the club re-opened to have everything ready. Mr. Rawe honored my request, giving us over three weeks of time off to travel.

On these vacations, we continued our travel by motor homes. When motor home rental got too expensive, we bought and pulled a 23-foot trailer with a full-sized Chevy van. This was a great way to travel since you can leave the trailer at the campground, while you tour in the van. We visited every state in the United States - except of course Hawaii.

For these camping trips, we purchased a little freezer. Before we left town, we bought steaks, shrimp and lobster tails from my favorite purveyors. I also pre-cooked many items - like meat sauce - at home for quick meals. We ate very well. One of the items my family really enjoyed eating on the camping trips was **Mrs. Harrison's Sweet and Sour Marinated Slaw**. Sweet and tangy with a satisfying crunch, the slaw was - and still is - a crowd pleaser. We had tablecloths, china and silver on the picnic table for our meals. In those days I was not familiar with California wine, so we bought gallon jugs of Inglenook wine for $7.45 from the club. We generally had about 20 gallons of wine for three-week vacations, but we didn't drink it all ourselves. We used it to befriend the neighbors in the campground. Sometimes we'd pull into the campsite late, so I'd ask a neighbor if I could use their already-hot grill. And then we had some wine together afterward.

One year we decided to tour Canada. At the border crossing, the customs agent asked if we had any *liquor*. "Yes," I told him, "We have a bottle of Crown Royal and a bottle of Sweet Vermouth." Another guy approached us, repeated the same question, and asked to search the vehicle. There were bench seats with storage in the motor home. He lifted up the seats and found our wine. I tried to explain to him it was wine - not liquor. I disclosed that we had additional bottles of wine in other cupboards in the motor home. He instructed me to bring all of the wine out of the vehicle. He charged us a $50 fine, and forced me pour the wine down the drain - all 20 gallons! He added that he could have confiscated the motor home - if we had owned it - but we were safe since it was a rental. It was a very dry trip, and it was harder to make friends in the campground that summer.

Back at the club, every February, club members elected new board members and a new president at the club. On election day, we had "freebies." Whenever something was free, *everyone* came to the club. We generally served a buffet with a roasted steamship round, which is about 60 pounds of a hindquarter of a cow. One year I found a corned steamship round. Corned beef remains red even when it's well done. Some of the members didn't like "rare" meat. Despite my explanation about the corning process, they told me to cut it only from the outside, which is definitely not the way to cut a steamship round; it should always be cut vertical to the bone. It was a corned failure.

When I first announced I was moving to Columbus, my friends warned me that Columbus was a "hick" town. It was another way of saying that people in central Ohio didn't have very refined culinary taste. In my first year at the club we served beef, fish, shrimp, salad, a lot of seafood and other common American staples. Side dishes included green asparagus from a frozen two-pound box and the "fancy" twice-baked potato. During the winter months, it was nearly impossible to purchase fresh herbs at the beginning of the 1980s, but I found a small farm in Michigan that shipped me little bundles of fresh herbs for $4 each. After a year or so, the members began to warm up to my menus. As they developed more demanding palates, we had to serve more than just prime rib and steak.

So we began a tableside service. We bought a *gueridon*, or a rolling table with a burner, for $1000 at a restaurant show. As the member watched, the waiter prepared and finished Steak Diane, which is two little sautéed tenderloins served with a cognac sauce. The steak was cooked in a skillet and then removed. To make the sauce in the same pan, the skillet is deglazed with cognac, then some demi-glace and butter are added. Finally, the sauce was poured over the tenderloins. We also cooked a tableside Pepper Steak using an eight ounce New York Strip Steak. Another favorite was Veal Oscar - two veal medallions with two pieces of canned white asparagus and two split shrimp with Hollandaise sauce on top. We proudly tossed a tableside **Caesar Salad** the traditional way with garlic, egg yolks, olive oil, lemon juice, and anchovies. Eventually members were ordering the **Pâté**, which I had started to make - something the hamburger-loving crowd wouldn't have touched in earlier years.

In 1981, I attended the ACF national convention. While there, I saw an ad for fresh chanterelle mushrooms, which I had never seen in the states before. I called the vendor, who lived on the West Coast of the U.S., to ask if the chanterelles were all the same size. No, he described them as yellow and wild grown, and told me that the minimum purchase was 18 pounds because they shipped in banana boxes. We were still pretty conservative at the club, so I wasn't sure whether I could use that many mushrooms. I called Chef Hubert at The Gourmet Market to tell him he could buy nine pounds of mushrooms from me. The chanterelles were shipped from Washington/Oregon for $7 per pound. My Veal Oscar was upgraded with chanterelles and was absolutely delicious. You see, I slowly educated the club members to try different foods.

On Saturdays in the Stag Bar, we had a somewhat regular 10am group who liked to get out of the house. They came for Bloody Marys. I also served them *Steak Tartare* or a Philadelphia Pepper Pot or Smoked Salmon. All in all - pretty classy.

At the Athletic Club, the main problem I faced was keeping the kitchen clean. When I first arrived, I hired Ecolab to provide the soaps and detergents. (I worked with Ecolab throughout my career.) We then purchased a power washer. Every Friday night after the dinner service was finished, the whole crew was required to stay and wash the kitchen. We donned rubber boots and hosed down the kitchen from top to bottom. First we scrubbed the walls and floors with soap. Then we rinsed everything. Luckily the well-built kitchen with its tiled walls and floor drained very well, and the room just sparkled when we were finished.

In 1983, I completed my Master Chef certification at the Culinary Institute of America (which I'll abbreviate in this book as CIA) in Hyde Park, New York administered by the ACF certification program. I paid my own tuition of $2,500 and all expenses, and the club kept me on the payroll. I only mention it here to show again how the club supported my career growth.

At the club we catered a lot of special parties. I got to know the members better, and they got to know me. Some of them were hunters, who brought their ducks for me to cook. However, the first time the ducks arrived with all their feathers. I had to clean them, but I only did that once! I told them I would be happy to cook their ducks - as long as they arrived cleaned. Some of the members weren't very skilled hunters, and the breasts were shot away or small bits of pellet remained in the meat. I declined to accept responsibility for any broken teeth.

In 1985, Mr. Rawe announced his retirement, and a new manager was hired. Around that same time, The Greenbrier began to recruit me. They invited me to judge their apprenticeship graduation in November 1985, so Margot and I spent three or four days there. It was a very classy place. In January I had an official interview. Back at the club, I wasn't particularly impressed with the new manager. So I was planning to leave the club anyway when The Greenbrier made me an offer. Around the first of March, I gave two week's notice to the Athletic Club. Then I started at The Greenbrier on March 15, 1986. When I left the club in 1986, I was the highest paid chef in Columbus at $56,000.

Marinated Sweet and Sour Slaw
(Mrs. Harrison's Special Recipe)
Yields 12 Portions

Ingredients

2 lb White Cabbage, tough outside leaves removed, cored and sliced very thin
1 cup Onions, fine chopped
1 cup Granulated Sugar
1 cup White Wine Vinegar
¾ cup Vegetable Oil
1 Tbsp Coleman's Mustard
1 Tbsp Celery Seeds
to taste Salt

Method

1. In a large bowl (stainless steel or China or glass), layer the cabbage, onions and all but 2 tablespoons of the sugar, in several alternating layers, ending with some of the onions.
2. In a sauce pan combine the remaining ingredients and bring to a boil.
3. Pour the hot dressing over the cabbage mixture.
4. Cover and put in a refrigerator for 24 hours – toss once or twice while chilling and again just before serving.
5. Serve cold or at room temperature.

Caesar Salad
Yields 2 Portions

Ingredients

2 each Garlic Cloves, cut in half
1 each Tempered Egg Yolk
1 tsp Salt
4 Tbsp Extra Virgin Olive Oil
2 Tbsp Lemon Juice
to taste Freshly Ground Black Pepper
1 head Romaine Lettuce, chopped
1 oz Parmesan Cheese
2 oz Croutons (garlic or plain)
(optional) 4 anchovy filets or strips of smoked salmon

Method

1. Rub a wooden salad bowl with the garlic using a fork. Add the egg yolk and a little salt and mix well.
2. Add the olive oil very slowly, a little at a time, constantly stirring with the fork to create a mayonnaise style dressing. Add the lemon juice.
3. Adjust the seasoning with the rest of the salt and pepper.
4. Toss the romaine in the dressing and divide onto two plates.
5. Sprinkle with Parmesan cheese and croutons.
6. Garnish the plates with anchovy or smoked salmon strips if desired.

Pâté

Ingredients

1 lb Veal Meat, cut into ¼" cubes
1½ lbs Pork Meat, cut into ¼" cubes
1 lb Pork Fatback, cut into ¼" cubes
2 oz Fine Diced Shallots, sautéed and cooled
2 oz Minced Garlic
2 Tbsp Fine Chopped Italian Parsley
2 Tbsp Dried Thyme
1 Tbsp Dried Marjoram
1 tsp Ground White Pepper
1 Tbsp Kosher Salt
1 tsp Curing Salt
½ tsp Ground Cloves
½ tsp Ground Nutmeg
½ tsp Ground Cardamom
½ tsp Ground Cumin
2 oz Heavy Cream
2 oz Cognac
6 oz Cooked Lean Ham, ¼" diced
8 oz Fresh Foie Gras, ¼" diced, deep chilled
8 oz Fresh Small Mushroom Caps, cut into ⅛s and sautéed in butter, chilled
4 oz Raw Unsalted Pistachios
2 Tbsp Green Peppercorns (drained)

Method

1. Combine the veal, pork and fatback and run through Kitchen Aid meat grinder, using the large die. Change to the small die and run half of the mixture through the grinder again.
2. Place the meat in the mixing bowl of a Kitchen Aid and add all of the ingredients from #3 - #14. Using the paddle, mix everything very well at mid high speed for 1½ minutes. At medium speed, fold in the heavy cream and cognac - 20 seconds. Make a small patty with the mixture and sauté in a skillet to taste for flavor. If necessary adjust the seasoning.
3. Add the ham, foie gras, mushrooms, pistachios and green peppercorns. Mix well at medium speed.
4. Using saran wrap, shape the mixture into 2½" logs (for plated appetizers) or 1¼" logs for Hors D'oeuvres. Use at least 7-8 layers of Saran wrap per log. Tie the log on one end with butcher's twine, and rolling back and forth while putting a lot of pressure on it, tie the other end.
5. Cook the large logs in a sous vide circulator at 140 degrees F for two hours. Small logs should be done in 1 hour. If you don't have a sous vide circulator, use a pot big enough to accommodate the logs comfortably and keep the water temperature at 140 degrees F as best as you can. Make sure to keep an eye on the thermometer. When done, place the logs in an ice bath and chill. When cool enough to handle, rewrap in saran wrap and place in the refrigerator. The pate can be store refrigerated for 3-4 weeks. In case you don't want to cook all of your pates at once, you can freeze some in the raw stage (already rolled into logs) and cook at a later date. Defrost before cooking.

Steak Tartare
Yields 6 Portions

Ingredients

1 lb Lean Beef (NY strip, top round or beef tenderloin), processed through meat grinder with small die
1 each Whole Egg
1 each Egg Yolk
2 Tbsp Canola Oil
3 Tbsp Fine Diced Red Onions
2 Tbsp Chopped Italian Parsley
1 dash Worcestershire Sauce
to taste Salt
to taste Freshly Ground Black Pepper

Method

1. Place all of the ingredients in a stainless steel bowl. Using two dinner forks mix well.
2. Serve with rye bread or sliced French bread.

Notes

Some recipes call for for chopped capers and cornichons, which is okay when the steak tartar is served immediately, but if the steak tartar is held over for a time, the meat will turn grey from the acidity.

The Greenbrier

What the guest requests, the guest gets. Never mind what.

I didn't leave the Athletic Club for the money; The Greenbrier only offered me a little more than what I had been earning in Columbus. Given the fact that I had far more responsibilities in my new position, it really wasn't a big raise. However, at this time The Greenbrier had a five-star Mobile rating, a five-diamond AAA rating and all kinds of other accolades. It was one of the finest resorts in the United States - absolutely first class - and I wanted that on my resume.

The Greenbrier is an expansive, luxury resort in West Virginia's countryside on the outskirts of White Sulphur Springs. Since this village, with a population of about 2,500, has very few eating establishments, the resort provides its guests with several onsite dining options. In the years I was there, The Greenbrier's main dining room seated 650 people. It was split down the middle by a stage where live music - mostly piano and violin - played nightly. This grand dining room normally served only breakfast and dinner. When we were extremely busy, though, we also offered a lunch buffet there. The Tavern Room had a special, much smaller menu for really fine dining. Four chefs worked closely packed into a small kitchen to service this venue. The Golf Club served small, continental-style breakfasts as well as lunch and dinner. For the first couple of years I was there, we had a wonderful lunch buffet complete with ice carvings in the Golf Club. Old White was a cocktail bar above The Tavern Room with a live music trio. Later in the evening part of The Tavern Room was converted into a disco with a disc jockey to try to draw a larger crowd, but this venue just wasn't well utilized. The guests were very active during the day - golfing, horseback riding, swimming, skeet shooting, hiking and playing tennis and yard games - and after dinner they were done. They didn't sit around in the bar much. Kate's Mountain, on the other hand, was a popular spot. It was an outdoorsy dining venue that served up to 500 people. Guests were transported there by bus and limousine because it was too far to walk. Sometimes we held pig roasts at Kate's Mountain with three full pigs butterflied on a trailer barbeque. Later, barbeque guru Steven Raichlen taught some cooking classes there. Draper's Café, aptly named for the resort's former decorator Dorothy Draper, was a coffee shop that served breakfast and lunch. It was also a venue used by guest chefs for special dinners.

Dorothy's protégé was Carlton Varney. He was the interior decorator while I was at The Greenbrier. Carlton had a say in everything related to décor - dishes, silverware, place settings, flowers and more. He was quite flamboyant and very good at his job. Years later, when Carlton visited Columbus as a guest speaker for the Franklin Park Conservatory's Hat Day, I invited him to our restaurant. He noticed a bare wall, and told me he had some beautiful pictures that would be just perfect there. When I asked for more information about this artwork, I discovered that each picture was about $35,000. I thanked him, and told him I wanted to wait a little bit. Exquisite taste comes with a big price tag!

Moving to The Greenbrier was a big change for me because it was just so different from my other jobs. It took me about nine months to adjust to working there, to get a handle on the whole situation. I worked from 8am until 9pm - unless there was a special dinner and then I worked later. I never took an afternoon break because I was busy developing new recipes and had all kinds of projects. There was never a dull moment.

My office was perched above the kitchen, so I could oversee the whole kitchen from my desk. I had a loud-speaker system, which meant that I could hit the button and ask someone to come up to my office. I also used the loudspeaker to give orders. Twice a day I rounded to check all the venues. In the morning I rounded at Draper's and The Golf Club, shaking everyone's hand along the way as my morning greeting. In the evening, I took role call in the main dining room with the wait staff. During this time, I talked to the servers about what was on each plate, how it was prepared and how it should be served. Then I rounded for about an hour at The Golf Club, The Tavern Room, Kate's Mountain and other party venues in the hotel. Although I was still involved in food production, I mostly inspected the food for quality and the kitchen for order. There were a lot of chefs and staff to oversee.

I went from a small crew of 25 at the Athletic Club to an army of 250 at The Greenbrier. I had 65 chefs and 12 pastry chefs, along with six bakers, three butchers, dishwashers and kitchen cleaners. Furthermore, all of them belonged to a union, which was a new experience for me. The unions had so many rules, which I always tried to observe. In the five years I worked there, the hotel only had to hire a lawyer once. One of my employees wanted a morning shift and I wouldn't give it to him, so he filed a grievance. When I left The Greenbrier, the union representative thanked me for teaching the chefs and the waiters. I wouldn't have had it any other way.

I am a hands-on chef - I like to help. For example, if we needed to plate a large party, I would be the one cutting the meat. This is a bit unusual. Generally the executive chef *directs* such activities, but he doesn't participate. One of the reasons I did that is I wanted to show the other chefs how to properly and expertly handle the position.

At the Athletic Club we had a conveyor table, which is a very efficient tool for plating. The plate comes down the conveyor belt, and each item that goes on the plate is handled by one individual: meat, potato, sauce, vegetable, garnish and lid. I told my boss at The Greenbrier, Mr. Rod Stoner, that we could keep the plates cleaner - because people did not have to handle them - and plate faster if we bought a conveyor table. In 1986 he purchased a plating table with two adjustable-speed conveyor belts, which they still use to this day. You could run it and - bang, bang, bang! - the plates were ready. They were ready so fast that you had to have at least three people at the end of the line to put the plates into the hot boxes. On New Year's Eve, we served about 1,400 guests in the ballroom. We were able to plate all 1,400 meals in 45 minutes! Our serving line ran like a well-oiled machine.

The bake shop, on the other hand, was sometimes not quite as efficient. They just couldn't seem to have the muffins ready at 6am. One of the reasons that the muffins were not done on time was that the bakers didn't always show up at 4am. I soon fixed this and, from then on, we always had muffins ready on time.

My teaching also extended to the apprentices in our two-year apprenticeship program. These apprentices, however, were not fresh-out-of-high-school individuals. They each had already graduated from a three-year ACF apprenticeship program or a culinary school. The Greenbrier offered a great opportunity for them to practice and hone their skills in every kind of cooking through rotations in all of the resort's kitchen stations. When they arrived on April 1, the apprentices were given their entire schedule; every three weeks like clockwork, they moved to the next station. However, my scheduler and executive *sous chef*, Steve Mengel, was occasionally short on one station, so he'd pull an apprentice to help. For example, one day, I asked one of the apprentices in the bake shop, "What are you doing down here? Aren't you supposed to be on the sauce station?" He replied, "Mr. Mengel sent me here instead." This was unacceptable to me; I wanted our apprentices to experience the full benefit of their rotation schedule. We had a responsibility to our apprentices just as much as they had responsibilities to us.

Each year we hired between 8 and 10 apprentices. In order to graduate, second years - also known as seniors - were tested on cold food display platters, hot food plates, a tallow piece (which is a decorative sculpture made from a beef fat and wax mixture) and an ice piece. (While the ice piece originally served the very practical purpose of keeping the food chilled in a warm room, with the advent of air conditioning, ice sculpting morphed into an object of beauty rather than a necessity on the buffet table). For the hot food segment, they had to prepare a four-course menu, with ten servings of each course. They were given a mystery item - usually a protein - and they had two hours to produce 16 plates. Then we brought judges in to evaluate their dishes. The young chefs earned medals or certificates, which were presented to them at the formal black tie, gold service graduation dinner in the evening. At this multi-course meal, they feasted on all sorts of wonderful dishes, including our succulent **Rack of Lamb** and **Stuffed Barbecue Quail on Green Lentil Ragout**. In addition, the hotel invited the seniors' parents for a complementary two-night stay at the hotel for the graduation. Following the gold service dinner, many of us headed to White Sulphur Springs' bar, *The Black Bear*, in our black-tie attire. There we mixed with the locals in their blue-collar attire. Graduation was always bittersweet. While we welcomed some of the graduates to the Greenbrier to begin their careers, we also said goodbye to some fantastic talent.

I was very proud of my program's zero drop-out rate. The only apprentices that we lost during my tenure were one who was killed in a car accident and another who was fired due to drug problems.

You cannot mention the apprenticeship program without praising Chef Hermann Rusch of Switzerland, who came to The Greenbrier from New York around 1957, because he was instrumental in the program's inception. He was the first person to ask, "Why don't we educate our own local people at The Greenbrier instead of bringing everyone from Europe?" The Greenbrier treated Chef Rusch like a king. They threw him an extravagant 80th birthday party with 250 guests and a giant cold buffet in the shape of the Swiss flag. He was a real gentleman. He always said, "We are ladies and gentlemen serving ladies and gentlemen."

I first met Chef Rusch in Frankfurt in 1980 at the Culinary Olympics. When I arrived there for the individual competition, the organizers found my name on the list and pointed me to the American team's booth. Chef Rusch, an advisor for the team, was in the booth guarding the food. As I approached the booth, Chef Rusch inquired, "Who are you?" I explained that I was an individual competitor from the United States. Chef Rusch was very protective of his team's food and didn't want me in the area. But before he shooed me away, he asked me, "Where are you from?" I was wondering then if he was perhaps interested in recruiting me. I have always wondered if he played a role in bringing me to the Greenbrier.

Chef Rusch loved to golf, but he didn't take it too seriously. When it came to putting, he used "gimmes" as long as the distance to the hole was less than the driver's length. The Greenbrier had three golf courses: Lakeside, Old White and The Greenbrier. One day we played all three courses - 54 holes! We started at 9am, grabbed two sandwiches along the way for lunch and were done in time for dinner.

But before we finished, the golf carts ran out of electricity, and we had to walk the last two holes. The man had so much energy.

For many years, Chef Rusch also ran the food service operation for the athletic Olympics. Chef Rusch retired from The Greenbrier in 1977. He and his wife lived in a beautiful home in Lewisburg, West Virginia. Eventually, he suffered from a blood clot in his leg that wasn't diagnosed soon enough, and his leg had to be amputated. This just wrecked him, and he passed away a few years later. He was very special to me.

Chef Rusch trained a person who was really a big help to me there - Jim Ambrosh. Jim, originally from Wisconsin, came to the Greenbrier in 1966 for his apprenticeship under Chef Rusch. He stayed there until he retired in 2004 as the director of catering. Whenever I needed help, information or advice, Jim was the person to consult. One big advantage he had was he did his apprenticeship with Mr. Stoner, so he knew Mr. Stoner very well. Everyone in White Sulphur Springs knew Jim and Jim knew everyone in White Sulphur Springs. He lived in a very nice house right outside town, where he loved to entertain. As a matter of a fact, he arranged a silver wedding anniversary party for Margot and me. In 2007, he moved to Florida, but we still see each other occasionally and talk on the phone.

Another relationship I cherish is the one with my immediate boss at The Greenbrier - Mr. Stoner, the food and beverage manager and a Greenbrier apprenticeship graduate. Mr. Stoner had been there for quite some time and not every day was a "sunny" day. However, he taught me so much, and I give him a lot of credit. He knew how to handle a big property with enormous volumes. He knew how to plan parties of any size and how to talk to the client. He taught me The Greenbrier's golden rule of hospitality: What the guest requests, the guest gets. *Never mind what.*

Every year we spent hours developing a book called *The Repertoire*, which contained myriad menus for every function you can imagine - from breakfast to meeting breaks to dinner and parties. We offered regular dinners, gold service dinners, special dinners and much more. In addition to the dining venues I already described, we also had party venues, including a large ballroom for 1,200 people, (where we often served many appetizer portions of **Seafood Sausage** and **Saga Cheese and Crabmeat Fritters**, festive favorites among our guests), the *Chesapeake Room* for 400 people, the *Crystal Room* for 250 people and parlors for any size parties. The guest would read *The Repertoire*, and then ask, "What else can you do for us?"

One year in April, we hosted the American Express Convention for about 1,600 people in two groups of 800. American Express contracted a full three-ring circus - complete with elephants and acrobats - for the convention. The circus tent was about a mile away from the hotel, and they requested that we serve dinner in the circus tent during the show. So we cooked everything in the hotel, put it in hot boxes and plated the meals in the kitchen tent adjoining the circus tent. Normally April is a very nice month, but this particular April it snowed and it was extremely cold in that circus tent. We tried to heat the place with air pipes that forced warm air into the tent, blasting the air on the highest setting until the tent gave the impression that it might just float away. We plated as fast as we could and served 800 hot meals that evening. That was The Greenbrier - what the guest wants, the guest gets.

Chef Mengel was a Greenbrier apprenticeship graduate as well. He played a critical role as my staff scheduler, which was particularly challenging in the spring and the fall when occupancy fluctuated. Since staff salaries were fairly high, Mr. Mengel carefully constructed the schedule each week to have just enough staff. It took him at least three days at the end of each week to prepare for the following week. He had to take all events - cocktail parties, special dinners, everything - into account, and naturally we had to be flexible during the week and alter the schedule, if necessary.

The season was normally about eight months, from Easter through November. October was a busy month, but by the second week of November things slowed down, and it stayed slow until a couple days before Christmas. People arrived in time for Christmas and most of them stayed 12 days. In the slow months of January and February, the count was very low. Mr. Mengel had his work cut out for him with the schedule!

The housekeeper was Mrs. Houser. She was a tough woman, who did an incredible job managing the entire resort, including the 720 guest rooms and all public spaces. Everything was perfect. The curtains, sheets and table linens were clean and crisp. The rooms absolutely sparkled. And she knew exactly what was going on at any given moment everywhere in the resort.

Every day the top management - the president, the general manager, the food and beverage managers and all the other key people - ate lunch at a round table at *Draper's Cafe* together to discuss the current activities. About 65% of our business was conventions/groups; social business accounted for the remaining 35%. Our management preferred the group business because it was more profitable. Needless to say, group business was also extremely demanding for the staff.

During my first three months, The Greenbrier provided me with lodging. I lived in one of the hotel's older cottages. It was nothing special. In fact, I shared the space with mice; I used to find tiny teeth marks in my bath soap. During those months, Margot and Susi (Kirsten was already in college) stayed in Columbus to finish the school year. I drove to Columbus every week or two to visit. I left on Friday evening at 10pm and arrived in Columbus by 4am. It was a six-hour drive on back roads as there was no highway in those days. Two days later, I left Columbus at 4am and was back at The Greenbrier by 9am in time for work on Monday. Lucky for me, I don't require much sleep.

I became very health conscious while I was there. The Greenbrier's beautiful indoor pool inspired me. Every morning, I got up early, made a quick bowl of oatmeal that I shoveled down with cold milk, and drove to the club to swim before work. I swam one mile every day - even on Sundays - for about three years. I always swam breast stroke because I don't know how to swim free style and maybe would have drowned. Then I showered and shaved in the locker room. I dressed in my uniform, which I brought with me on a hanger, and then I headed to work. We also had a gym and I walked on the treadmill, which became almost an addiction for me. Exercising at the Greenbrier was an opportunity I just couldn't resist.

Margot and Susi moved to White Sulphur Springs in June. Poor Susi was not happy to be there. She had just finished the sixth grade in the Upper Arlington schools in Columbus, and she was so far ahead of her class in White Sulphur Springs, West Virginia that she really didn't need to study. She never had homework because she already knew the material. One day, I arrived at work at my usual 7am, and noticed that Susi was still sitting in the car when I got there. I asked her why she didn't remind me to drop her off at school. She explained that she just didn't want to go to school because she already knew everything that they were teaching.

She always carried a brown bag lunch to school with her. Margot packed a nice ham and cheese sandwich for her. Susi began to ask for a peanut butter sandwich instead. "The other kids make fun of me for eating for eating ham and cheese," she complained. On another day, the kid next to her in class was chewing tobacco and she told him it was bad for his teeth. They exchanged some angry words and then she called him a "redneck." Margot said, "You can't call him that," to which Susi replied, "You should hear what he calls me."

Episodes like this made her lose interest in school. So Margot went to talk to her teacher. The teacher offered to put her in a gifted program for two hours a week. A special teacher came from out of town to teach the gifted class, but that idea did not satisfy Margot, who wanted Susi to skip a grade. The teacher wasn't convinced, so

Margot talked to Susi's former Upper Arlington teacher, who agreed to write a letter to compare what Susi had already learned to what she was currently learning - in support of Susi skipping a grade. The school finally agreed on the condition that if it didn't work, Susi would go back to the lower grade. Things began to improve for Susi - especially when she got to the high school in Lewisburg. Susi graduated when she was just 17 and really enjoyed her time in West Virginia.

When Margot and Susi first arrived in West Sulphur Springs, we began searching for a place to live. We discovered that real estate was extremely expensive in that area, so we rented a house about eight miles from the hotel. Perched on a hillside, the house had a beautiful location with sweeping views of the entire valley. It was spacious enough with a living room, a dining room and four bedrooms. We loved the cozy fireplace and the big porch was perfect for parties. The gravel road that led to the house was steep and had a deep ravine on one side. When we had a party, as the guests were leaving, I stayed on the porch to count the cars as they entered the main road - to make sure no one was in the ravine.

In January 1987, we had a major snowstorm. I couldn't make it home from work because we lived on a private road that wasn't plowed by the town. My secretary, Diane, was married to George, who had a snowplow, so he plowed a little for us. For the next few days, I had to leave my car at the bottom of the hill, and walk the mile to and from my house each evening and morning. I was young and energetic, and it was good exercise. But then I got smart, and bought chains for the tires of one of the cars. Each day I used two cars: I drove the chained-tire car to the bottom of the hill and then hopped in my other car to drive to The Greenbrier. In the evening I reversed it.

And we didn't just have trouble with snow. Water was a problem at first too. The house had running water that was fed by pipes that ran *above* ground from the highway. It was an odd design, but the water ran... and ran evidently. Our first water bill was $15,000! I complained to the mayor and he said, "The meter doesn't lie." But I insisted on an inspection, and they found - and repaired - a leak. We didn't pay that bill.

We quickly learned that there were no secrets in White Sulphur Springs. If I sneezed down in the village, by the time I drove to the hotel, the staff had already heard that I had a cold. I was once driving on I-65 near Lewisburg, West Virginia. I needed to fill my gasoline tank, so I exited the highway and I didn't exactly stop at the top of the exit ramp. A highway patrolman pulled me over. I told him that I had stopped - a gentle, rolling stop. The police officer used his radio to call in my driver's license. Everyone in the area had a police scanner and one of my sous chefs heard that I had been pulled over. He called Chef Mengel, who called our daughter, Kirsten, in Columbus to tell her that I had been pulled over by a state trooper. And when I arrived in Columbus, Kirsten was so upset, wondering what had happened.

There was one big secret, though, at The Greenbrier. After I had been there about one year, Mr. Stoner told me to report to the building where the television repair crew worked. What I learned that day was: the "television crew" was just a cover up. It turned out The Greenbrier had a bunker under the clinic building that was built in the 1960s during the Cold War. In case of atomic war, U.S. government officials - both the House of Representatives and the Senate - would arrive by train. The bunker's meeting rooms were designed with a fake backdrop to look exactly like the Washington Monument to fool the American people watching newscasts into thinking that the representatives and senators were still in Washington, DC. There was a radiation decontamination chamber. There was enough food to feed everyone for six weeks, mostly dehydrated and canned foods as well as a lot of tomato products. The bunker was fully stocked just in case something happened. It even had a dentist office.

When I arrived in the bunker's office that day, I was greeted by Central Intelligence Agency (the other CIA) officials, who wanted me to read a document and sign on the dotted line, making me the official chef in case of war. It was top secret. I couldn't even tell Margot. I had to cook a meal for about 50 people in the bunker every six months with three of my cooks, who had also signed the CIA document. We had to make sure everything was in working order.

Our scheduler, Chef Mengel, wasn't very happy about taking chefs off the schedule for unknown purposes. When I requested three chefs every so often, he asked me, "Why? What are you doing?" Given the secrecy enshrouding the bunker, I wasn't allowed to explain. I said things like, "None of your business" and "I just can't say!" He always had to acquiesce because he reported to me, but he certainly wasn't happy about it. In 1993, a reporter from *The Washington Post* wrote about the bunker, and the secret was out.

Mr. Stoner soon told me that he was hiring an assistant manager from one of our properties in Saint Croix as an apprentice. Although I didn't like the idea, the assistant manager came anyway. This guy had never cooked before or at least not much, but he took everything very seriously. For example, when he was supposed to create vegetables garnishes for a hot plate, he actually used a Black and Decker drill to make a tunnel through a carrot, slid an asparagus into the hole and then sliced the carrot into medallions. That's a crazy amount of work for a garnish. I called this practice "food engineering" instead of cooking. He later dropped cooking and specialized in ice carving, and he has a great business in Florida.

Our ice carvings were not up to snuff when I first arrived. I had heard about a talented ice carver, Mac Winker, who had published an ice-carving book. I didn't know anything about carving a 300-pound block of ice myself, but I hired Mr. Winker to give an ice-carving seminar for all the apprentices and me. He taught the basics. The ice block must be crystal clear. You must mark the ice using a stencil, and then you begin working with the chain saw. He could make a gorgeous crystal vase in about 20 minutes. During the seminar I learned so much that afterwards I was able to carve Rudolf and all of his reindeer friends for Christmas.

During my time at The Greenbrier, I got involved with cooking demonstrations. Throughout the winter months, Julie Dannenbaum came monthly from Philadelphia to teach a week-long cooking class to 65 or so people - mostly women. The participants arrived on Sunday afternoon, and we gave a reception for them in the evening. Over the course of the week, we also brought in famous winemakers and guest chefs for one day like Jacques Pepin, Dean Fearing (who demonstrated his fantastic **Barbecue Seasoned Oysters** recipe), Marcel deSaulniers, Julia Child and Jeremiah Tower (who prepared delectable **Vegetables Cooked Two Ways**). Thursday evening we served the famous gold service dinner with the china and flatware all trimmed in gold. Many of the participants' husbands arrived later in the week for the gold service dinner and stayed through the weekend, and they all went home Sunday.

On one occasion in the winter of 1987, our students arrived and we had our cocktail reception on Sunday as usual. The class was slated to begin on Monday morning. I organized the logistics, provided all the ingredients and loaned Julie one of my chefs to assist her. However, this particular Monday morning, Julie received tragic news of the death of 2-year-old grandson. She was absolutely crushed. Of course Mr. Stoner let her go home, then asked me to take over the class. Well, I had never cooked her dishes before, and I had certainly never talked to a roomful of 65 women and men. However, I had no choice and taught the class. I lived from one session to the next.

During that week, I learned a lot of lessons - maybe more than the participants. First, a demonstration is show business. You have to talk constantly. You do not stop talking or they start having conversations among themselves. Second, you must have lots of your food prepared ahead of time - or your audience loses interest while you're just peeling and chopping. Third, don't give them a chance to talk. You must tell them all sorts of stories while you are doing your demonstration. If they start talking, you can just forget it. I survived the week. Only one woman dropped out.

Her reason: she had come especially to see Julie - not me.

When The Greenbrier began to offer four cooking classes a month, chef and cookbook author, Anne Willan, came and taught the classes in her lovely British accent. Her class drew lots of people. On Tuesdays during her class, we always brought in a guest chef, including Larry Forgione, Anne Rosenzweig and Mary Sue Milliken of the television show "Two Hot Tamales." I was the Thursday chef during Anne's classes, and I demonstrated the gold service dinner, which they would have the opportunity to enjoy that evening. This experience proved to be very beneficial for me later in my career, and I'll tell you more about that soon. One year we had a guest chef / "food stylist" from Chicago. She was on the board of the CIA with Mr. Stoner, and she thought she knew everything. She wanted to set up a buffet with a whole cooked salmon, and I didn't want to do that. I preferred to skin and fillet the fish, cut it into small serving-size pieces, poach the pieces and "re-create" the salmon - piece by piece - on the platter. Otherwise, the fish looks terrible as soon as three people help themselves. So I refused her request. A few hours later, Mr. Stoner called me because she had complained to him about my rude behavior. He asked me, "What are you doing to me? She wants the whole salmon." Although I told him it wouldn't work, in the end I agreed. I provided her with a perfectly-prepared whole salmon. I didn't dare look to see what happened to it after it left my kitchen.

As an executive chef, it is very important to ensure that only top quality food is used in the kitchen. Bob Corey and his brother owned a produce company in Charleston, West Virginia and they were our main produce supplier. Charleston is about 130 miles away from The Greenbrier, so our produce arrived at least three times a week on a truck. One day, I was downstairs when the deliveries were unloaded. We always ordered a whole pallet of Driscoll's strawberries. Driscoll's has an A label and a B label, and we insisted on A-label strawberries. B-label berries were of no interest to us. But that day, I noticed that we received the B label. When I saw this, I told the driver to load everything back on his truck and return it to Mr. Corey. I said, "Tell him we don't accept B label here; we only want the good stuff." He took the whole truckload back to Charleston. Bob Corey is very good businessman, who felt that I had educated him that day. We became good friends.

To this day, I still have fond memories of some of the chefs. For example, our *potager*, or soup chef, was Shack. His job was to cook all of the soups. His ***Five Onion Soup with Toasted Shallots and Fresh Chives***, a velvety smooth, creamy delight, amazed our guests with its silky texture and bold onion flavor. He had been there forever - more than 35 years. Shack had a room all to himself with all the steam kettles, and in his room he also had a little desk with a little drawer. Although the drawer was always padlocked, I knew that he had a couple bottles of beer in there. One day we were expecting the health inspector for our semi-annual inspection. I told Shack that he had to open up his drawer, so the health inspector could make sure everything was nice and clean. The health inspector arrived, Shack disappeared and the drawer was locked. After the inspector was gone, Shack acted like nothing had happened.

One of Shack's more challenging responsibilities was to prepare the consommé for the gold service dinner. We traditionally served this highly-regarded clear soup instead of a puree or cream soup, so our guests felt comfortable at this the multi-course meal. We served the soup in cups with a gold rim and golden soup spoons. The spoon sparkled in the soup when the consommé was perfectly prepared. It must be crystal clear. I explained my consommé expectations to Shack this way: "If you take a penny and put it in the bottom of a 5-gallon bucket and fill this bucket with consommé, I should be able to read the year on the penny." He replied, "Yes, chef." He could be quite agreeable.

Once in a while, though, Shack had a bad day and his soup was not particularly clear. I reminded him about the penny and added, "I could not read the year on the penny with last night's consommé." His response was memorable, "Chef, I think maybe you need some glasses."

My four breakfast chefs were all locals, born and raised in White Sulphur Springs and trained in The Greenbrier's apprenticeship program. This breakfast crew boasted 140 years of combined service at The Greenbrier. One chef, Kenny Carter, poached about 400 eggs every afternoon and reheated them the next morning for service. He was truly a master at his profession. Another chef prepared beautiful omelets. A third chef made fantastic fried eggs - over easy and sunny-side up. The fourth chef prepared other breakfast items. Plus they had one or two apprentices to assist them. These four key people on the breakfast line could have done their jobs in the sleep - even if they'd been out the night before. Breakfast was never a problem.

Hunting season, however, was sometimes a little problematic. It starts the Monday after Thanksgiving, and it's a big deal in West Virginia. Even the schools close for a week because the children hunt too. For example, I had to give some of my bakers a week off to hunt or they would quit, so the bakery was short-staffed. And so was room service during bear-hunting season. The room service waiters were bear hunters. They fed the bears apples all summer and fall, and as soon as the hunting season opened, they shot their well-fed bears.

In addition to hunters, we had a farmer at The Greenbrier. Pete Alderman was a great person, our senior *saucier*, and a product of The Greenbrier apprenticeship program. He was a farmer when he wasn't working at The Greenbrier, but whenever he was in the kitchen, he could do whatever you needed to have done - never mind what.

Lawrence McFadden is a great chef and was a Greenbrier apprentice when I first arrived there. Later he was promoted to *saucier* and then *sous chef*. He married a girl from White Sulphur Springs, and they moved around the world together. He worked at the Waldorf Astoria in New York; The Intercontinental in Chicago; The Ritz Carlton in Naples, Florida and became corporate executive chef for the Ritz Carlton corporation eventually; the MGM in Las Vegas, which he quit after just nine months (I predicted that wouldn't work for him anyway); and the Shangri-La in Hong Kong, a very exclusive chain based in Hong Kong with hotels in the Far East, Paris and Toronto. Then he moved to Singapore to be the CEO of a culinary school. He is now the general manager of The Union Club of Cleveland, which is closer to his wife's family.

I also fondly recall Kenny Boone, the *entremetier*, or the vegetable chef; Boula, the vegetable-shaping artist, who took over for Shack as *potager* when he retired and is still there today; and Eric Crane, the executive pastry chef, who was at The Greenbrier for 30 years or more. He and his 12 pastry chefs made tortes, cookies, bread puddings and all sorts of desserts. Eric was not particularly worldly, but he had a special talent: he designed, created and decorated huge chocolate Easter eggs and jaw-dropping wedding cakes. He was also very skilled at simpler desserts. He prepared a delicious **Almond Tuille** that he formed into a basket shape and filled with seasonal berries and whipped cream. I know I occasionally annoyed him when I suggested new ways of doing things. He was defensive saying, "We don't have the Culinary Olympics here every day, Chef." Once, his 80-year-old mother was invited as a guest to the gold service graduation dinner. Her perfectly coifed hair and stylish gown gave her an elegance that I found quite charming. She approached me and said, "Chef, you must be nice to my Eric." I found myself somewhat tongue-tied. I smiled and obediently said, "Yes, ma'am." I may have been a little easier on Eric after that.

Chris Muller from Wisconsin was *The Tavern Room chef*. In 1988 he was my apprentice for the national team, and went to Frankfurt with me. He was also a driver when I travelled to the CIA for practice sessions. Chris got in the VW Golf, put his earphones on and drove... really fast. I made sure he knew that he had to pay for his own speeding tickets. He worked for a couple years in Washington, DC and later he became the *saucier*, the *sous chef*, and today he is the *chef de cuisine* at Le Bernardin in New York City with Chef Eric Ripert.

I traveled quite a bit, and every time I had to travel, Mr. Stoner always asked, "Do you have to go again?" He didn't leave the Greenbrier too often, but at least once a year for the hotel show in New York or the restaurant show in Chicago in May. Otherwise he didn't see too much of the outside world. I thought I brought a lot of new ideas back to the Greenbrier from my travels. I think it was very beneficial to them, but Mr. Stoner didn't see it that way at first.

But things were changing. The owner of the Greenbrier was CSX Corporation, a railway and shipping company. In 1986 CSX bought RockResorts with properties in the Virgin Islands, Hawaii, Vermont and Wyoming. Mr. Stoner was promoted to vice president of food and beverage for all of the properties, and in this role he had to travel to the properties. It was very eye opening for him. He began to develop an understanding of the importance of travel and seeing new things. When I needed time off to travel, he was more understanding.

It is interesting to note that the other benefit of CSX owning The Greenbrier was they started The Greenbrier Express, which was the American version of the Orient Express train; it ran from Chicago to White Sulphur Springs to Washington, DC. They had really old railcars that were beautifully equipped and decorated. After The Greenbrier Express was discontinued, some of its cars were parked in Washington, DC and others in White Sulphur Springs. The cars were used for private parties that were catered by The Greenbrier staff.

In 1991, Margot and I decided to return to Columbus to open our own restaurant. Mr. Stoner was very upset when I resigned on May 15, 1991, but later on after my departure, he invited me back for the apprenticeship graduation as a guest and judge. I felt both honored to attend and pleased that Mr. Stoner was no longer angry. We invited him to Columbus for a master chef dinner, and we have enjoyed a good relationship ever since. I must have done something right at The Greenbrier. Sadly, Mr. Stoner is no longer at The Greenbrier, and you can sense the difference.

After my departure, Chef Walter Scheib came to The Greenbrier from Florida as the executive chef. Later, he secured the executive chef position at The White House under the Clinton administration. He worked for the Clinton administration, and the first term of the Bush administration.

I saw Walter several years ago at a Greenbrier fundraiser for the cancer center in Morgantown. In fact, all of The Greenbrier's former executive chefs were invited for this event - Mr. Stoner, Peter Timmins, Rich Rosendale, Robert Wong, Walter Scheib and I. We each cooked one course for 350 people. Robert, who owned a restaurant in Charleston, West Virginia, collapsed a few weeks later on the tennis court and died at age 50. Peter Timmins, who worked at The Greenbrier for ten years, took a position at the Gasparilla Inn and Club in Florida before he moved to the Everglades Club, just north of Palm Beach. I saw him in October 2014 at an Electrolux seminar in Charlotte. Four weeks later, he was shot and passed away at the age of 57. In 2015, I received a call that Walter had died. He had been hiking in New Mexico and fell in a ravine; the rescue team found him dead three days later. He was 61. I was deeply saddened by these tragic young deaths.

Rack of Lamb
Yields 8 Portions

Ingredients

For the lamb
2 each 8-bone Rack of Lamb, 24oz each
to season Salt
to season Freshly Ground Black Pepper
2 Tbsp Olive Oil
2 Tbsp Very Finely Chopped Garlic
1½ Tbsp Fine Chopped Fresh Rosemary
to taste Salt
to taste Freshly Ground Black Pepper

For the rosemary cider sauce
2 cups Apple Cider
½ each Guajillo Chili (may substitute with dried red chili pod)
2 Tbsp Dark Brown Sugar
1 each Rosemary Sprig

For the vegetables
2 Tbsp Extra Virgin Olive Oil
2 Tbsp Unsalted Butter
1 Tbsp Finely Diced Garlic
8 each Baby carrots, peeled, cut in half and blanched
8 each Fingerling Potatoes, cut in quarters lengthwise, pre-cooked
8 each Yellow Squash Batonettes, 2" long each, blanched
16 each Sugar Snap Peas, cut in half on the bias, blanched
3 Tbsp English Sweet Peas, blanched
3 Tbsp Short-cut (on the bias) Green Onions
1 each Roasted Red Bell Pepper, peeled, seeded & cut in julienne
to taste Salt
to taste Freshly Ground Black Pepper

Rack of Lamb

Method

1. Season the lamb racks with salt and pepper.
2. In a heavy duty skillet with hot olive oil, sear the racks on all sides. Remove from the skillet and let cool a little.
3. Sprinkle the garlic, rosemary and a little more salt and pepper on the lamb racks.
4. Place the lamb racks on a glazing rack on top of a sheet pan. Put in a 400 degree F preheated oven and roast for approximately 20 minutes.
5. Remove from the oven and let rest for 5 minutes before serving.
5. In a heavy sauce pan, bring the apple cider to a boil and reduce by ½.
6. Toast the chili, then break it apart by hand and add it to the cider. Add the brown sugar and rosemary and bring back to a boil and reduce by 1/3.
7. Strain the sauce through a chinois, cover with plastic wrap and keep at room temperature until ready to serve.
8. Place the olive oil, butter and garlic in a skillet and sauté gently. The garlic should not have any color.
9. Add the vegetables, season with salt and pepper and toss to warm.

To Serve

1. Equally distribute the vegetables on 8 plates, in a small mound towards the top of the plate.
2. Cut each rack of lamb in 8 pieces and lean two pieces on each mound of vegetables.
3. Drizzle the sauce over the lamb and around the perimeter of each plate and serve immediately.

Stuffed Barbecue Quail
on Green Lentil Ragout
Yields 6 Portions

Ingredients

For the quail
1 each Bacon Slice, small diced
¼ cup Small Diced Onion
¼ cup Small Diced Celery
¼ cup Small Diced Carrots
¼ cup Small Diced Granny Smith Apple
¾ Tbsp Finely Minced Garlic
½ Tbsp Finely Minced Jalapeno
1 cup Stale, Small Diced Sourdough Bread
1 each Egg White, lightly whipped
as needed White Stock
6 each Quail, partly boned
4 Tbsp Barbecue Sauce

For the green lentil ragout
12 oz Dry Green French Lentils
1 each Bay leaf
4 Tbsp Olive Oil
3 oz Carrots, small diced
3 oz Celery, small diced
3 oz Onions, small diced
½ Tbsp Minced Garlic
1 Tbsp Jalapeno
1/3 Tbsp Chopped Fresh Rosemary
1/3 Tbsp Chopped Fresh Thyme
1 each Bay Leaf
as needed Chicken Stock
to taste Salt
to taste Freshly Ground Black Pepper

Stuffed Barbecue Quail
on Green Lentil Ragout

Method

1. Render the bacon. In the bacon fat, sauté the onion, celery, carrot, apples, garlic and jalapeno.
2. Add the sourdough bread and mix thoroughly. Let cool a little.
3. Season as needed.
4. Mix in the lightly whipped egg and enough white stock just until the mixture is moist.
5. Adjust the seasoning as needed.
6. Fill the stuffing into the quails. Season the quails with salt and pepper and place in a skillet.
7. Brush the quails with barbecue sauce and roast in a 400F preheated oven for 8 minutes.
8. Serve on the green lentil ragout.
9. Soak the French lentils for 4 hours in cold water; strain.
10. Cook the lentils in salted water until done (about 20 minutes). Strain the lentils and wash under cold running water.
11. Sauté the carrot, celery and onion in olive oil until translucent.
12. Add the garlic, jalapeno, fresh herbs and bay leaf and cook 2 more minutes.
13. Combine the lentils with the mixture above.
14. Add some chicken stock and bring to a boil.
15. Reduce to low heat and simmer for a few more minutes.
16. Remove and discard the bay leaf. Adjust seasoning with salt and pepper as needed.

Notes

*3 oz of small diced Tasso ham and 3 oz of small diced andouille can be added.

Seafood Sausage
Yields 12 Portions

Ingredients

½ lb Flounder, fresh
1 lb Shrimp, raw, 26/30 count
1 lb Scallop, raw 10/20 count, fresh
2 Tbsp Dill, short cut
1 tsp Worcestershire Sauce
to taste Salt
1 tsp Cracked Black Pepper
to taste Lemon Juice
2 each Egg Whites
2/3 cup Heavy Cream
1 oz Whole Unsalted Butter, room temperature

Method

1. Dice all of the seafood into small pieces - less than ¼".
2. Take 1/3 of the seafood mixture and put it into a food processor. Place the other 2/3 of the seafood mixture in a bowl and fold in the fresh dill, Worcestershire sauce, salt and black pepper. Mix well.
3. Purée 1/3 of the seafood mixture in a food processor, adding first the egg white (one a time), then the heavy cream in three stages, then the butter and a little salt until you have a very smooth texture.
4. Remove the mixture from the food processor and mix with the 2/3 of the diced seafood mixture. Check the flavor.
5. Using Saran Wrap, create 1 ¼" logs and tie on both ends. Poach at 140F for approximately 20 minutes. Remove the logs from the hot water and place in an ice water bath to chill. Slice to the desired size and shape.

Notes

If your flounder and scallops were frozen, you need to double the egg whites!

Saga Cheese and Crabmeat Fritters
Yields 30 pieces

Ingredients

6 each Egg Yolks
½ cup Milk
1 cup All-purpose Flour
6 each Egg Whites
5 oz Saga Cheese, diced or crumbled
1 lb Crabmeat
to taste Salt
to taste Freshly Ground Pepper
1 quart Peanut or Canola Oil

Method

1. Using a wire whip, mix the egg yolks with the milk.
2. Fold in the flour.
3. Whip the egg whites with a Kitchen Aid to a soft peak. Fold ¼ of the whipped egg white carefully into the above batter to lighten the mixture. Fold in the rest of the egg whites.
4. Fold in the saga cheese and crabmeat.
5. Place the oil in a pot and heat to 360F.
6. Using two soup spoons, shape the batter into quenelles and drop into the hot oil. Deep fry until golden brown.
7. Remove from the oil with a slotted spoon and place on a paper towel. Serve with Sauce Louis.

Barbecue Seasoned Oysters
on Red Onion and Spinach Salad
Yields 6 Portions

Ingredients

For the Oysters:
2 Tbsp Paprika
1 tsp Ground Cumin
1 tsp Ground Coriander
1 tsp Dark Chili Powder
1 tsp Sugar
1 tsp Table Salt
½ tsp Fine Ground Black Pepper
½ tsp Ground Thyme
½ tsp Curry Powder
½ tsp Cayenne Pepper
½ cup Flour
24 each Medium-sized Shucked Oysters
1 cup Clarified Unsalted Butter or Canola Oil

For the Red onion and Spinach Salad:
½ cup   Sweetened Rice Wine Vinegar
1 Tbsp   Sugar
to taste Salt
1 each   Medium-sized Red Onion, peeled, cut in half and julienned
1 each Small Carrot, peeled and julienned
1 ½ cups   Fresh Spinach Leaves, julienned

For the Blue Cheese Dressing:
1 cup Sour Cream
1 cup Mayonnaise
1 ½ cups Crumbled Blue Cheese
¼ cup Buttermilk
to taste Salt

Barbecue Seasoned Oysters
on Red Onion and Spinach Salad

Method

1. Mix all of the spices with the flour.
2. Put the oysters in a colander and then on a paper towel to dry them a bit.
3. Lightly coat the oysters with the seasoning mix and shallow fry them with the butter or oil in a heavy bottomed skillet; about two minutes on each side.
4. Serve immediately on the red onion and spinach salad with blue cheese dressing.
5. For the salad, put the vinegar, sugar and salt in a small pot and bring to a boil.
6. Have the onion julienne in a stainless steel bowl and pour the boiling vinegar over the onions. Cover with saran wrap and let the onions marinate and cool.
7. At service time mix the marinated onions with the carrots and spinach julienne.
8. For the dressing, whisk together the sour cream and mayonnaise.
9. Stir in the blue cheese.
10. Thin with buttermilk to the desired consistency.
11. Season with salt and pepper to taste.

To Serve

Take 6 - 10" plates and put on each plate 4 small piles of the spinach and onion salad. In the middle of the 4 piles put 2 tablespoons of the blue cheese dressing. Place one shallow fried oyster on top of each pile of spinach and onion salad. Serve immediately.

Vegetables Cooked Two Ways
Yields 6 Portions

Ingredients

12 each Baby Carrots, trimmed and peeled
6 oz French Haricot Vert Green Beans, both ends trimmed
8 each Spring Onions, trimmed and peeled
1 each Yellow Squash, cut in large julienne
1 each Zucchini, cut in large julienne
1 each Small Red Bell Pepper, cut in large julienne
1 cup Chicken Stock
4 oz Unsalted Butter
2 Tbsp Chopped Fresh Parsley
½ Tbsp Chopped Fresh Dill
½ Tbsp Chopped Fresh Basil
to taste Salt
to taste Freshly Ground Black Pepper

Method

1. In a skillet and covered with a lid, start cooking the carrots and haricot verts in the chicken stock. After a couple of minutes, add the rest of the vegetables that don't require as much cooking time (keep the skillet covered). All of the vegetables should be cooked al dente when the chicken stock has evaporated.
2. Remove the lid and the skillet from the heat and add the butter and herbs. Fold the vegetables into the butter/herb mixture until they are evenly glazed; season to taste with salt and pepper.
3. Serve immediately.

Note

As an alternative, you can also blanch the vegetables in boiling salted water until al dente, transfer to a stainless steel bowl, and then toss with the butter and herbs and season to taste).

Five Onion Cream Soup
with Toasted Shallots and Fresh Chives
Yields 12 Portions

Ingredients

½ lb Shallots, sliced
½ lb Leeks, sliced
1 lb Red Onion, sliced
1 lb Spanish Onion, sliced
2 bunches Green Onions, cut short
2 ½ quarts Chicken Stock
to taste Salt
to taste Freshly Ground White Pepper
½ quart Heavy Cream, scalded
3 each Shallots, sliced thin and fried crispy
2 Tbsp Short-cut Chives

Method

1. Put first six ingredients in a soup pot and cook until all onions are tender.
2. Let cool a little, then place everything in three batches in a Vita Mix blender and purée very smooth.
3. Put everything back in a clean soup pot. Reheat and add the scalded heavy cream. Adjust the seasoning if necessary.
4. Garnish with crispy fried shallots and short cut chives. Serve immediately.

Almond Tuille Shells
with Seasonal Berries and Sauce Anglaise Amaretto
Yields 36-40 small shells or 18-20 large shells

Ingredients

4 oz Unsalted Butter, melted, not too hot
5 oz Granulated Sugar
5 oz Light Corn Syrup
5 oz Sliced, Blanched Almonds, not too fine and not too coarse

Method

1. Melt the butter and mix together with all of the ingredients. Stir once in a while until the mixture is completely cold.
2. Preheat the oven to 320F and bake on a Silpat or parchment paper until golden brown. Remove from the oven and let cool a little. Mold over glasses or other containers to the desired shape.
3. Mixture yields 36-40 small or 18-20 large shells. Per large shell use about 2½ oz of seasonal berries and 2 oz of sauce anglaise amaretto.

Culinary Competitions

At what I thought was the right moment, I asked him if the club might be willing to sponsor me to participate in the Culinary Olympics as an individual competitor.

Throughout my career as a chef, I thoroughly enjoyed participating in cold food competitions, which were all the rage until the mid-1980s. At first blush, though, cold food competitions can seem a bit strange. Here are some odd facts about such competitions:

- We prepare food that is for display only and cannot be eaten because it is prepared up to several days in advance and is heavily glazed with aspic to preserve the food. After the competition, you just throw it away.
- You use more product than you display, so you have a lot of waste.
- You spend a lot of time during practice sessions with no immediate results.
- You prepare hot food that is displayed cold.
- To achieve excellent results, you place each small food item on a toothpick and dip it in aspic. (The only type of food that you don't glaze is breaded or dough items as they get soggy.)

On the positive side, cold food competitions provide the chef with a chance to:

- Experiment and develop new presentation techniques;
- Explore new ideas and recipes;
- Develop new display platters with interesting shapes;
- Work with other chefs and exchange ideas; and
- Attend international shows, where you discover new ingredients and different eating cultures.

The most positive part of cold food competitions is that they teach you discipline, challenging you to pay attention to details and cleanliness. Without these factors, you don't earn any certificates, medals, honors or money. These skills learned in the competitions become a regular part of your everyday work, making you a better chef. Also, through the competitions, I had the great fortune of working with some of the best players in the culinary world for many years - especially on the U.S. National Culinary Olympic team in 1988 and the ACF regional team in 1984. Without participating in competitions, I don't think I would be as good a culinarian as I am today.

Around 1988, hot food competitions became popular. At these competitions, preparation time is shorter and the work is less labor intensive. Plus, there is less waste and an emphasis on flavor as well as presentation.

My culinary competitive career started in 1980. As I mentioned before, I grew up in Schotten, 50 miles north of Frankfurt, where the culinary competitions have been held for more than 100 years. Nearly 1,000 chefs participate in the *Olympiade der Koeche*, or Culinary Olympics, every four years. I lived there again from 1970-1977. Although the Culinary Olympics were held in 1972 and 1976, I had neither the drive nor the funding to participate then. I did, however, work at the trade show that took place at the same time as the Olympics selling Philips microwave ovens.

In 1980, when I was established at the Athletic Club in Columbus, I invited my manager, Mr. Rawe, to our home for dinner once in a while. Since Mr. Rawe was originally from Bremen, Germany, we talked over dinner about our home country and the Culinary Olympics there. At what I thought was the right moment, I asked him if the club might be willing to sponsor me to participate in the Culinary Olympics as an individual competitor. Without hesitation, his answer was, "Why not? Make a budget for me." I was so excited! I submitted my budget which included a plane ticket, a rental car and food. I had a free place to stay with friends and access to a free kitchen. I also would be away from work for nine days with full pay. I knew since the Athletic Club was a private club, they could not use this for marketing purposes. The only thing they might get out of it was keeping their executive chef around for another few years. I was pleased that my employer valued my work that highly.

I called my brother, who was still working in the Bahamas, and asked him if he'd like to join me. He'd have to pay his own way. He said, "Sure, why not!" I planned to display on Monday with Category A and my brother would display on Tuesday with Category B. I would display again on Wednesday with another Category B. I really wanted to make the most of it. I outlined roughly what I wanted to cook/display, and I ordered some mirrors and chinaware for the food display from a friend. Chefs with money used silver display trays; poorer ones - like me - used mirrors. A meat purveyor, Marc Sarrazin of DeBragga & Spitler in New York City, agreed to donate one prime rib, one strip steak, four racks of lamb and one beef tenderloin. Margot's friend, Edith, had an uncle named Werner, a *Kuechenmeister*, or certified master chef, who had some show experience. He agreed to be my adviser. I was all set.

One day before my departure, I had seven lobsters delivered to the club. I cooked them and wrapped them tightly in wet towels and plastic wrap. On the day of my departure, I put the lobster between my clothes in my suitcase and hoped for the best. I had a layover at Kennedy Airport, where Mr. Sarrazin met me with the donated meat in a wheeled suitcase - the first such luggage I had ever seen. I landed in Frankfurt at 6:30am and walked through the green line at customs without being stopped. I was so relieved because you weren't allowed to bring any food into Germany, and my two suitcases were stuffed with meat. I drove to Schotten and put everything in the walk-in cooler there. I met with my advisor, the *Kuechenmeister*, to make some concrete plans. This was my very first competition since my petit four display as an apprentice at age 17, and I had not practiced anything in preparation for this competition.

The next morning, Friday, I drove to Frankfurt to shop for supplies, and then we started cooking. We worked until late Friday night, continued again early Saturday morning and all day Sunday with almost no sleep. Now here comes the kicker. My brother, Hubert, who was supposed to arrive on Friday, showed up Sunday afternoon with a cooler full of meat, but told me that he was too tired to compete. He suggested we have a barbeque party after the competitions were done to use his meat. That was my brother.

Since I had registered him for Tuesday, I felt responsible to take his place and show food on his spot. So now I was displaying three days in a row! We worked Monday until 5am, then I loaded the car, drove 60 miles to Frankfurt, set up the display, drove back to Schotten to cook for the next day, drove to Frankfurt the same evening to break down the display, returned to Schotten to work all night and drove to Frankfurt to set up the next morning, Tuesday. And then I repeated this on Tuesday and Wednesday. I may have slept a total of four hours in six days. On Wednesday morning after I set up, I had to pull over and sleep in the car on the side of the road for two hours. I was *kaput*.

When I went back Wednesday evening to attend the awards presentation, I won two bronze medals! As a special prize, I received a Hutschenreuter china espresso set, which I still own. Whenever we use that china, all of the memories of my first competition come flooding back to me. When I returned to Ohio, everyone was excited that I had done so well. My apprentices wanted to know everything about the competition. They indicated that they would like to participate as well on a local level.

One person who was interested in competing was my *sous chef*, Uwe Rudnick. I had recruited him from the Bahamas and the club had sponsored his green card.

Uwe was a lot of fun. He changed girlfriends like I changed my uniform. Occasionally we invited Uwe to dinner to our house on Sundays when the club was closed. On these occasions, he always brought his girlfriend *du jour* along. Many of his girlfriends played with Susi. But, when one particular woman didn't, Susi complained to him, "Why didn't you bring your *other* girlfriend?" When Margot went to Germany for six weeks every summer, Uwe and I liked to go out for a beer together after work. He drove a red convertible, and sometimes it was hard to remember where we parked. He knew a little bit about competition. He knew a little bit about Culinary Olympics. And he showed a little bit of interest in participating.

When the local chapter from the ACF staged the first competition in Columbus with Categories A and B, a grand buffet category, a small buffet category and a pastry display category, Uwe and I entered the competition. Uwe made a *pâté en croute*, which requires very careful slicing to ensure you display the design. Well, he started cutting the *pâté* on the wrong end. To compensate for the mistake, we had to doctor it up with a wide ribbon and a bow. I won a grand prize with a trophy. Uwe won a trophy as well.

In May, there was always the National Restaurant Association (the other NRA) show in Chicago on Lake Michigan. My first time there, I took an apprentice with me to help unload and set up. At this event you had to be set up at 5pm for judging, and at 4:45, I noticed there was still an empty table. At 4:55 a chef arrived carrying one platter. Two guys followed him with one platter each. The food on those platters was absolutely perfectly displayed. This chef was Richard Schneider, one of the first certified master chefs in the U.S. and a team member of the 1980 Culinary Olympic team. Naturally, he earned gold and best of show. For just my third competition, I did quite well too. I displayed in the A and B categories, and won silver in A and bronze in B. The display right next to mine that year was a chef from Dayton, Ohio with a fancy silver platter. He put a raw red snapper on the platter. The next day you could not go near that table without gagging - it smelled so awful.

A couple years later, there was another bad display by a gentleman from Toledo, Ohio. He called his display "Beaver in the Mudpie." On the platter was a skinned, butterflied beaver with buckteeth and feet still intact, lying on a puree of black beans surrounded by hard boiled eggs that were cut in half. Chef Rusch, a judge that year, exclaimed, "Oh my god, oh my god!" just before he shoved the entire platter under the table.

For the next several years, as I continued to compete, I included my apprentices more and more. We participated in competitions in the region around Columbus - Pittsburgh, Chicago, Detroit, Cincinnati, Cleveland and New York City. I never will forget our first competition in Cleveland at the West Side Market in June. The market was kind of an open building with butcher shops and vegetable stalls. When you arrived there at 4am, you were greeted by the pungent aroma from the garbage cans. Before we left Columbus, we did not have time to apply a second coat of aspic to our food items. As inexperienced as I was, I said we'd take the aspic along and do the second coat in Cleveland. However, at 4am it was already close to 80 degrees - too hot to apply aspic. Even with this setback, we earned silver and bronze. In addition to the medals awarded at the competition, Minor International awarded a $200 scholarship every year for the best apprentice display. I am proud to say that my apprentices won this award four years in a row.

At every competition for the next couple of years, I earned silver in A and bronze in B. It came to the point that Margot said, "Are you ever going to earn gold?" That did not sit very well with me. So I sought advice from various chefs, including Richard Schneider, who called me a "Dumb So-and-So". He advised me to do *one* category well, and I'd be successful. I took his advice and dropped Category B. At the next competition, I won gold in the A category. *Thank you, Rich!*

Trips to Chicago were always very special. Four to six apprentices traveled there with me. (I couldn't take everyone or the Athletic Club kitchen would have been empty.) The apprentices prepared food for platters. I lined up the platters for display and judging. Our platters always won medals. I set some competition ground rules for the apprentices: 1) Keep the material cost as low as possible. Don't waste anything. 2) Work only when the club is closed - through the night or on Sundays. The Chicago competition started on a Saturday, so Friday night we worked all night and left Columbus early Saturday morning.

We were always leaving late for Chicago. On one of these trips, just a few miles out of Columbus, we passed a police officer who was in the oncoming lane. We had a radar detector, but it doesn't help you when no one else is on the road. He put on his bubblegum machine lights, made a U-turn over the median, and pulled us over. He was nice and polite, as he asked, "What are you doing? Where are you going?" I was nice as well as I answered all his questions. I thought I had talked myself out of the ticket, but that was not the case. I got a $50 ticket.

The McCormick Place location in Chicago had a challenging loading dock. A policeman stood at the end of the ramp to make sure there were only three cars at the loading dock at one time because space there was very limited. We were in line, waiting to unload. We had everything on sheet pans in a box of ice to keep it cold. The car's air conditioning was running as cold as possible in an attempt to keep the food chilled. That policeman just wouldn't let us on the ramp. Now, at past competitions, I always had beautiful flower arrangements - red roses with white gladiolas - on my display table that I gave to the woman in charge of the competition salon when the events were over. As it turns out, this proved to be a strategic hospitality move. I hopped out of the car to find her. Then I asked her for a 20-minute extension since we'd been waiting for 45 minutes to unload, and needed time to set up. She happily granted my request. That became our regular routine - until they hired a new girl.

I later found out during my time at The Greenbrier that chocolates work as well as flowers to charm and calm people. We had three girls at The Greenbrier who did nothing but make chocolate truffles and treats. Whenever I traveled, I took a couple of boxes of chocolates with me. (It's too bad my rich, velvety **Chocolate Terrine** didn't travel well!) They worked magic at conventions. I recall a particular birthday party for Chef Rusch at The Greenbrier, where quite a few colleagues and chefs were invited. The party started at 1pm with champagne and a lunch buffet. One chef came from Virginia with his fiancée. I showed him around the hotel, but his fiancée didn't join us on the tour. When we returned to my office, she was not there. In fact, she was nowhere to be found. The chef said, "I'm leaving. I'll just leave her here." And he went back to Virginia without her. About 30 minutes later, she showed up in the office a little tipsy. She started whining and complaining to me. "You chefs, you're all the same," she said. I said, "Okay, but he's gone. I can get you a hotel limousine and a box of chocolates. You just tell the driver where to take you." She actually smiled when I handed her the chocolates. I don't know whether she married the chef or not.

In 1983 the ACF was looking for its 1984 Olympic team. The tryout had two segments and took place at the Conrad Hilton Hotel in Chicago on Michigan Avenue. First, you had to score at least silver in the cold food display to be invited to the hot food tryout. I set up my display and went back to the Harrison's house, where I was staying. The judges said they would call if I made silver and was eligible to participate the next day in the cold food tryout, but no call came. The next day I found out that I had only scored a bronze medal. However, I didn't give up after this setback. I continued to compete on the regional level instead.

Chef Fritz Sonnenschmidt, originally from Bavaria, and I had completed our Certified Master Chef (CMC) exam together a few months before. I stayed with him during the exam period - 130 hours of testing over a 10-day period. Every morning Fritz knocked on my door at 5am and called out, "Rise and shine." I showered, drank some coffee and headed to the examination. For classic cuisine, we had to cook exactly like *Le Guide Culinaire*, an enormous book of recipes. I had studied the whole book. A couple months later, Fritz approached me to join the regional New York team, which was not ACF-sponsored.

However, I only participated in one meeting in New York. During the 1984 ACF national convention in Orlando, Florida, Mr. Metz pulled me off the New York team and put me on his regional team to replace someone who had dropped out for health reasons. Naturally, I was very excited. In addition, at the last NRA show, my apprentice Carolyn Claycomb had qualified through a cook-off to be an apprentice for the ACF teams. That year the ACF had one national and two regional teams. Each team consisted of four chefs. Each chef had an apprentice. Since Carolyn had worked for me at the club, I convinced Mr. Metz to allow us to work together. I had some catching up to do because, while the other team members had already practiced a lot, I was new. Plus I had to become a U.S. citizen to meet the ACF requirements. Although I had been a green card holder since 1965, I finally became an American citizen in June 1984.

We had one more practice session at the Galleria in Dallas in August. My good friend, Victor Gielisse, was the executive chef there. Although this was my first session with the team, I already knew most of the team members from food competitions. I was warmly welcomed by everyone. Dan Hugelier presented me with one of his team jackets with American colors and a special logo. He said, "Since you're a team member, you should look like a team member." It was fancy, and I wore it proudly.

Mr. Metz was the team manager and Rich Schneider was the team captain. At this particular practice session, each team member was required to make a recommendation for the hot food plate. Rack of lamb was the given protein, but the team members hadn't decided yet how to prepare it. Because I was brand new, I didn't know the protocol for making a recommendation. Everyone brought a rack of lamb and cooked it there. I had cooked mine in Columbus and brought it cold. I didn't have any intention of re-heating it because I didn't realize they would taste it. The advisers, the manager and the captain were sitting around a table. I was one of the last ones to bring mine out. I explained what I had done and they nodded and said, "Uh-huh." Then I was allowed to leave. I was only halfway out of the room when I overheard Baron Galand say, "Who the hell wants to eat cold lamb?" That was shocking for me - I was very embarrassed.

At the end of September, it was time to leave for Frankfurt to compete. We wore matching outfits - gray pants, white shirts, neckties, burgundy sports coats and Western Stetson hats! Our group of 12 chefs and 15 apprentices sure looked American. We placed very well, earning all gold medals and one silver medal. The silver was earned by a pastry chef, who made a cornucopia full of mouth-watering marzipan peaches. He purposely created one half-rotten peach - since there's always one spoiled fruit in the basket. But because the judges didn't understand his philosophy, they awarded him silver.

After the judging, we packed our equipment - sheet pans and baking pans and lots of other stuff - into an airline container. I included a suitcase of my own equipment in the airline container, and we shipped it home. I stayed in Germany a few more days to visit our families in Baden-Baden and Schotten. When it was time to fly home, I couldn't find my passport anywhere. I realized it was in the suitcase that I had already shipped home! When I called the U.S. consulate in Stuttgart, I was told that if I could prove who I was and could fulfill the formalities, I could get a new one. I lost a whole day getting a new passport, but was eventually able to travel back to the U.S.

Although I returned to my routine of work at the club, I already had new plans and goals in mind: I wanted to be a 1988 national team member. Until this time, I had been on the regional team which only displayed cold food. The national teams cooked hot food in a restaurant setting. Carolyn, my *sous chef*, wanted to be a regional team member. Tryouts for the cold food took place in Charlotte, in Detroit and on the West Coast in1986. Carolyn tried out in Charlotte and I went to Detroit so we did not compete against each other, which turned out to be a good tactic. She traveled to The Greenbrier to help me with my set up. Then I traveled to Columbus to help with hers. Using this great plan, we both qualified for the 1988 U.S. team. There was also a hot food tryout in Chicago in May during the NRA show. After the hot food tryout, the team manager, Mr. Metz and the team captain, Chef Tim Ryan, made the final selections of members for the national team. However, I had one small problem: The ACF fielded a team for a Singapore competition, which took place one week before the Chicago tryout. It would be difficult to compete back-to-back on different continents.

First, let me mention a couple things about Singapore. In 1984, I shared a room with Chef Jeff Gabriel from Detroit. For the Singapore competition, we were required to bring centerpieces and Chef Gabriel's centerpiece was very fragile. Airports had just introduced x-ray machines. We were boarding a plane in San Francisco when the guy at the x-ray machine wanted to take the centerpiece out of Chef Gabriel's hand. Chef Gabriel went bananas. He cussed and carried on, but he was required to allow the centerpiece to pass through the machine. Somehow, it made it through unscathed.

In Singapore, the temperatures are extremely hot and humid in May. Preparing food with aspic in the heat is very difficult. We had three walk-in coolers, but one after the next, the coolers broke down. We were going in and out too frequently. Sigi Eisenberger was in charge of the hot food, displayed cold. He had to make six plates. Mr. Metz came in around 3am on the day of the competition and said, "We're not going to use this. You have to come up with something better." Now we really had to scramble. We had to make six different hors d'oeuvres on little glass plates. In the evening, we discovered we were short one dish... Gabriel said he had some troutlings from Michigan. "Why don't we bone these troutlings and stuff them with mousse?" We assigned the two apprentices with us to bone these tiny fish. One poor apprentice, who was tasked with this job, had the hiccups that lasted for several hours. Each time he tried to pull out a little bone, his body jerked with a hiccup, making this delicate job that much more difficult. At the awards ceremony, the outcome was a bit confusing. We won gold, but with the same number of points as the Canadian culinary team.

We flew from Singapore to Chicago, arriving Sunday at 7am. My Chicago tryout began Monday at 7am. For the salad course, I prepared a **Chevre Cheese Soufflé**. I went to the judges table to serve it out of a big soufflé dish, which was very impressive. On Wednesday morning when the results were announced, I was a member of the U.S. national team and Carolyn made the regional team.

The following years were the most exciting and rewarding years of my culinary career. It was an honor to work with such a talented and professional group of gentlemen. There were no *prima donnas* on our team. Learning from each other and working with each other was a real privilege. Mr. Metz served as our manager. Tim Ryan and Mark Ericson were very knowledgeable contributors. And Dan Hugelier - what a chef! - had mastered flavor, presentation and ice carvings. I was the oldest team member and Dan called me "Dad," so I called him "Son." Our pastry chef, Christopher Northmore, was absolutely first class with a clean kitchen, remarkable presentations and delicious flavor profiles. To this day, I call him for help if I need a dessert recipe. Whenever he sends me a recipe, he always puts this comment on it: "Even a chef can make this." I believe that the 1988 ACF National Culinary Team was the best team the ACF ever had. Mr. Metz encouraged us, inspired us and pushed us to the limit. He always said, "There is always room for improvement." His leadership made us all better chefs. I think I can speak for everyone on the team when I say this, *"Thank you, Mr. Metz!"*

At another international competition in Basel, Switzerland, we were serving duck and swordfish in two seatings. At the first seating, we didn't have too many diners, so we were generous with the portions. What we didn't know was that those who missed the first seating would come to the second seating. Mr. Metz wasn't there, but his brother was. So, it would have been bad if we had run out of food. Mr. Metz would have found out about it even before we were finished serving. In order to stretch our servings through the second seating, we went downstairs to a restaurant and purchased some smoked goose.

Participating in competitions like the Culinary Olympics requires managing challenging logistics and attending myriad practice sessions. Our first mission was to find a kitchen in Frankfurt for the team to work prior to the competition and to finish preparing everything. The kitchen had to be not only close to the exhibition halls, but also private. Otherwise we would be constantly bothered by the media, press, relatives and friends. (When you are competing in the Culinary Olympics, you would not believe how many friends you have all of a sudden!) Mr. Metz decided to send Tim Ryan, the team captain, and me to Germany to find the right location. He selected me because I spoke the language and knew the area, but Tim was there to make the final decision. We contacted several food production companies - like Nestle and Achenbach - beforehand and visited their kitchens. While they all had positive points, the negative points worried us. They were all too accessible to the public. One venue that we really liked, though, was the catering kitchen on the 34th floor of the Dresdner Bank. It was very spacious and boasted a clean environment and equipment. We talked to the executive chef of the bank, Chef Rudolf Decker, but he wasn't permitted to make such a decision - we had to talk to management. By fortuitous accident, I discovered that the Huntington Bank in Columbus did business with the Dresdner Bank in Frankfurt. Furthermore, the Huntington Bank had board meetings every so often at The Greenbrier. I also had met Mr. Frank Wobst, the CEO of the Huntington Bank at that time, on one of these occasions. The next time I saw Mr. Wobst at the Greenbrier, I approached him to ask if he could help us. After a short time and some correspondence, we landed our dream kitchen for the competition. There we experienced total privacy. Nobody could come to visit without clearance from security officers downstairs. It was just fantastic!

Our other goal on our seven-day visit to Germany was to find china and silver platters. I drove quite a few kilometers on that trip with Tim as my co-pilot. Tim was a little skeptical about my driving style at first, but he got used to it. Upon our return to the U.S., we reported to Mr. Metz, who was pleased with our work.

Once the national team was formed - after the 1986 tryouts - we had practice sessions every month or two at the CIA in Hyde Park, New York. Since White Sulphur Springs doesn't have an airport and the closest airport to Hyde Park is about an hour drive, I just drove to the sessions. In the beginning, I drove the 560 miles alone. I used to pack six delicious hard rolls from the bakery and slices of soft cheese with a 6-pack of Coke, and drive through the night directly to the practice session. Then, I realized that Freddy Tiess, one of my apprentices, was originally from upstate New York and his parents lived only ten miles away from the CIA. I asked Freddy if he'd like to go home for a weekend. "Sure!" he agreed. I told Mr. Mengel to give Freddy a few days off. I planned to make him drive, so I could get some sleep before the practice session.

I owned a manual-shift Volkswagen Golf GT. I drove all the way to Harrisburg before Freddy got in the driver's seat and admitted, "I don't know how to drive a stick shift." He was about to learn. I showed him the clutch, the brake and the gas. I showed him the gears. I showed where reverse was, and told him not to use it. Luck was with us as the gas station where we had stopped was on a hill. As we coasted downhill, I told him to press the clutch, put it in first gear and then give a little gas. We made it out of the gas station and onto the highway. Of course, now he needed to get into higher gear, so I helped him shift all the way to fifth gear. Then I asked, "Do you get it, Freddy?" "Yes, chef, I think so," was his not-too-certain response. I told him not to experiment and instructed him to wake me up before we exited the highway. We arrived without incident - maybe he did some praying - and I was even able to take a little nap.

Lawrence McFadden, a senior apprentice when I first arrived, also did some driving for me. Lawrence really liked to drive. When I was on the road, I really liked to eat Kentucky Fried Chicken. I had no idea that Lawrence didn't care for it. On the way home, we stopped and got out of the car at a KFC. He said, "I'll be back shortly." In about five minutes, he showed up with a Burger King bag. I guess he liked it his way.

With all my drivers, I had a driving rule: if you were driving and you got a speeding ticket, you paid for it. On one trip, we were about 10 miles from home, when we passed a yellow, unmarked car. Lawrence said, "Chef, I think you just passed the sheriff." So I slowed down, changed lanes and sure enough, I got pulled over. I never saw his flashers; they were in the grill. In Ohio, when you are pulled over you sit in the car and the police officer approaches your window. In West Virginia, however, the cop pulls out a bullhorn, and says, "Get out of the car!" I did, of course. Then he said, "I'm going to take you in." I was dog tired since we had just driven 500 miles. So, I simply nodded in agreement and hung my head a little. But I said, "I have AAA and they'll bail me out in no time." Then he asked me, "Who is the security chief at The Greenbrier?" When I told him the person's name, the conversation got friendlier: I only got a warning.

On another trip, Lawrence and I were driving through the night to a culinary competition in Pittsburgh. Actually, he was driving my van and I was exhausted, staring, sort of half asleep. We were going around a curve and I saw a sign coming right at me. I screamed. Lawrence jumped and said, "Chef, what's wrong?" Then he comforted me, saying everything was okay. Did you know that culinary competitions cause hallucinations?

Our last practice session before Frankfurt was in August 1988 at the CIA. We worked very hard all day Friday, Saturday and Sunday until noon. Afterward, we had lunch in a restaurant. To ease the stress from working so hard, everyone had to tell a joke. When it was my turn, I translated a joke from German to English. After the punch line, I was the only one who laughed. My colleagues asked me, "What's so funny about it?" I guess my translation wasn't very good.

Then we decided to play tennis. Tim, Mr. Metz, Mark and Dan were very good tennis players. I'm not a tennis player, so they gave me a racquet and some balls and told me to hit some practice balls against the wall. At one point, while hitting the balls, I must have tripped. I stumbled into the wall with my left shoulder. The pain was incredible. When I looked at my left shoulder, I could see the bone kind of pushing up on my skin. When the rest of the team took me to the hospital, I learned that I had broken my collarbone. There is not much that a doctor can do for a broken collarbone except pop it back into place and try to hold it in place with some bandages. Then I just had to hope that the bones would heal. Although I was supposed to be back at work at The Greenbrier on Monday, the hospital visit delayed our departure until 2am Monday. On the drive home, every turn and bump in the road hurt just awful. But when we made it back to the hotel, I put my left arm in a sling to rest my collarbone. Then things began to improve.

Since this accident happened just seven weeks before the competition in Frankfurt, my biggest concern was that I would be replaced on the national team. I called Mr. Metz and Tim every two days to tell them how much things had improved, to convince them that replacing me was not necessary. After three weeks, I was almost back to normal. Happily, I remained on the team. One week before the competition, we all left for Frankfurt.

We stayed at the five-star Hotel Frankfurter Hof, about three quarters of a mile from the kitchen at the Dresdner Bank. We were allowed to bring our spouses - which was something new. Mr. Metz thought it would lift the morale of the troops. Working on the 34th floor of the bank was fantastic. No one bothered us so that we could really work. One day we sent Chef Rusch - who was about 80 years old - grocery shopping. When he returned to the bank, the elevators were temporarily out of order. He called us to ask if we needed the ingredients right away. If so, he offered to walk the stairs - all 34 flights! We assured him that we could wait.

The Culinary Olympics always has an opening ceremony with a parade of the participating national teams. Each national team has a team mascot. That year, Mr. Metz chose Susi, our youngest daughter, to be our mascot. What an honor! But then we had to scramble to figure out what she should wear. Sometimes U.S. team mascots dressed as typical Americans - cowboys, Indians and the like. We decided that Susi would be the Statue of Liberty. Margot took care of getting the costume together, and Susi looked just great. But Susi, who was only 14 years old, decided she wanted to do more for the team than just serve as the mascot. Every day, she worked with the team from morning until late doing all kinds of chores like washing dishes and equipment, setting table for our meals, cleaning vegetables and more. I believe that this was when she decided to follow in my footsteps to be a chef.

Our diligent preparations paid off at the competition. In the cold and pastry competition we earned gold. In the hot food kitchen, we were pronounced world champions. One key to our success was that we combined classical, traditional cooking and display methods with modern culinary techniques. For example, we flew 5,000 pounds of ice from the U.S. to Frankfurt. Then Dan Hugelier, our ice-carving specialist, created a huge sunburst, which we placed in the middle of our cold food display table with platters and plates all around it. This is a very old, effective method to keep the food cold before there were refrigerated tables. Our regional team also did well that year - everyone earned gold.

In 1989 the South African Chef's Association celebrated its 25th anniversary and invited the U.S. and German National Culinary Olympic teams to Johannesburg, South Africa for a friendly competition. Both teams worked in the same kitchen. It was a great learning experience for all of us. The Germans had great glazing and casting techniques. To keep certain food items in a desired shape, they used cast bandages. First, they wrapped the food in plastic wrap. Then they casted it and cooked it in the cast. When they removed the cast, the food maintained a perfect shape. For example, they could shape a fish as it if were swimming. From the Americans, the Germans learned how to fully utilize everything. For example, for our 1988 squab entry, we used every last thing from that darn bird.

In 1990 a new team was selected. I decided it was time to take a new approach for competitions. From 1980 until 1989, I competed for medals and trophies. At the beginning of the 1990s, companies like Tyson Food, Ocean Garden, Certified Angus Beef, etc., started promoting their products through recipe contests with *prize money* involved. In 1990 and 1991, I participated in the National Seafood

Competition in Charleston, South Carolina and New Orleans.

In Charleston, I tried to please the judges by making an extra course - lemon sorbet. I thought it would be great, after eating fish all day, to cleanse their palates. Somehow, though, I must have made a mistake with the recipe. My electric ice cream maker was the "old-fashioned" kind with ice and salt. Although it ran for three and a half hours, the sorbet would not freeze. Chef Keith Keogh, the lead judge, eventually sent Victor Gielisse to my station to tell me to "shut the damn machine off". I came in second or third.

In 1991, I took a team of chefs and one pastry chef to Mobile, Alabama for the Mobile Gulf of Mexico Seafood Culinary Competition. Because I had selected some of the very best culinarians from The Greenbrier for the competition, we came in second place. The prize money was $10,000.

Then, in 1992, when I was living in Columbus, I put a team together called the "Tri-State Team" comprised of Victor Gielisse, a pastry chef from Dallas; Scott Bennett, *sous chef* at The Greenbrier and me from Columbus, Ohio. For the challenge, we had to cook a four-course meal for 50 or 60 guests. We had an excellent game plan, which included a salad course to be served with a cucumber sorbet. However, Chef Keith Keogh, again the lead judge, had a new rule this year: No ice cream makers. We found out about this one day before the competition. So we bought 10 pounds dry ice, mixed up the sorbet base and poured it into a two-inch hotel pan on top of dry ice. Naturally we could no longer call it sorbet, but rather granita. We earned gold and first prize - $15,000.

In 1993 and 1994, the ACF organized a recipe contest during its national convention. First, you submitted a recipe to qualify for your region - Northeast, Southeast, Central and Western. Then, the winner of each region was invited for a cook-off at the national convention. I entered Tyson's Wild Game and Fish as well as the Certified Angus Beef competitions. The convention started on a Saturday with the first competition at 1pm. Now it also happened that I was teaching a CIA course the entire week leading up to the convention - in Santiago, Chile. My course was finished Friday evening at 6pm. I flew to Miami, arriving at 10pm, Then, after a layover, I continued on to arrive in Orlando at 10am. My daughter, Susi, flew to Orlando from Columbus on Friday night with two big Styrofoam chests of ingredients that I had asked her to bring for the competition. After my arrival, I sorted everything according to the different competitions, and placed them on sheet pans on speed racks. At 1pm, we were ready to cook. Susi was my assistant and we worked well together. We had to prepare 12 portions of **Cornish Game Hen** in two hours. I had only practiced cooking this recipe once just two days before while I was in Chile. Even so, we won gold and first prize of $5,000.

Around that same time, I created another great recipe for Uncle Ben's Rice One Pot Cookery. It is a succulent **Shellfish and Rice Bouillabaisse** - a perfect combination of oysters, mussels, shrimp and scallops seasoned with fresh herbs, ginger and a bit of jalapeno.

The next competition was Certified Black Angus Beef. I decided to use a secondary cut of meat, the Spencer, or top blade, from the shoulder, which has great flavor and texture when it's cooked right. I had tried it a couple of times at home, but it took more than an hour and a half to get the meat tender. The only way to get it done and plated in the time we had was with the use of a pressure cooker. Since I had not tried this method before, we decided to make a practice run in our hotel room. We seared the meat, added the *mirepoix*, or diced vegetables, started the sauce the traditional way, put everything in the pressure cooker and then placed it on the burner. We did all of this in the bathroom of our hotel room. Once the pressure cooker was on the burner, we closed the bathroom door just in case... After 45 minutes we opened the door a little and peaked in. Everything seemed to be okay. We released the pot's pressure, opened it and tasted the meat. It was perfect. The next day, we cooked this at the competition and won another first prize - $1500. The third day, Wild Game and Fish was on the program, which we won as well: $4500. $11,000 in three days was not bad! At this convention, I was also selected by my peers as National Chef of the Year.

The following year, the national convention took place in San Francisco where they had all kinds of culinary competitions. Victor Gielisse decided to compete this year rather than judge. He was mad that I made all the money; he wanted to earn some too. I was not permitted to cook at the Tyson competition since I had won it the year before. So this year, Victor cooked... and ended up winning it.

The Certified Angus Beef was the first competition on Sunday. I arrived in San Francisco late on Saturday night. After unpacking, I discovered that I had forgotten some of my ingredients. I had rushed to the airport in such a hurry (after catering a wedding) that I left a whole tray of food at home. I had to go shopping at midnight, and had a really hard time finding everything I needed. One of the items was black beans, which must be soaked for several hours. The beans soaked that night in my room - in the hotel's ice bucket. Because of my poor preparation, I came in second. Victor won this one as well! Over the next few days, we placed either first or second in all of the competitions. We each went home with about $11,000. The only competition that we did not enter was the Uncle Ben's Rice One Pot Cookery: Ed Leonard won first prize, which was $1,000.

After our sweep in San Francisco, they changed the rules. One company said certified master chefs were no longer allowed to compete. Another company did not allow you to compete two years in a row. Therefore, I decided to take a break - which didn't last too long.

In 1994, I heard about the Grand Prix Culinaire International Auguste Escoffier in Nice, France. I thought this would be something different. Before you were invited to compete in Nice, France, you had to a win a tryout competition in your home country to qualify. I won the Auguste Escoffier U.S.A. Grand Prix competition, and went on to represent the U.S. in Nice. In preparation, I did some practice sessions in Chicago. Mr. Michel Bouit was responsible for organizing this in the States, and he provided me with a location where I could work in Chicago. He also found some French chefs in Chicago willing to critique my work. I was very fortunate to receive some really good feedback from French Pastry Chef Jacquy Pfeiffer, founder of the French Pastry School in Chicago, and French Chef Jean Joho from *Everest* in Chicago and others. The results in Nice were very encouraging. I won the dessert competition, and came in second overall.

In 1998, I was appointed by the ACF to be the manager of the U.S. culinary team. We had several practice sessions at various locations. Then, we took off for our first international competition at the Culinary World Cup Expogast in Luxembourg. We had a great team: we won gold medals in both the hot and cold food competitions. However, we had one major problem - no money. We were operating on a shoestring budget. Since I saw no improvement coming in this regard, I turned in my resignation after Luxembourg.

My next challenge was to participate in the Bocuse d'Or competition in 1997, which takes place every two years in Lyon, France. Here again, I participated in regional tryouts and then a final tryout in Chicago. The winner in Chicago would go on to represent the U.S.A. in Lyon. Our daughter, Susi, had graduated from the CIA a couple of years earlier and was working with Chef Eric Ripert at Le Bernardin in New York City. I decided she would be a perfect apprentice for me. The apprentice could not be older than 22 years, which worked in our case, since she was born in February 1974 and was still 22. Everything fell into place, and we were very excited to work together again. We registered for the regional tryout in Palm Beach, Florida. Although we did not have too much time for practice, we had a basic idea about what we wanted to prepare. Our main goal was to finish in the top three out of ten candidates because only the first three were invited for the finals at Kendall College in Chicago, Illinois. We finished in third place, and qualified for the finals.

For nationals we really had to prepare ourselves. Kendall College is a beautiful place, where I had competed in prior years. I was assigned to the same part of the kitchen that I had used in a competition that I had won a few years earlier. I thought this was a good omen. We drew numbers for the order in which we would cook and present, I drew number five (out of ten), which pleased me. In this situation you don't want to go first or second or last. You want to be in the middle so the judges have a better feel for what to expect. At least that's the position I prefer. Susi and I worked very hard for 5-1/2 hours. Our two platters looked great, our food tasted good and we finished on time. We snuck a look at the platters of candidates who followed us, and, in our opinion, they were not even close to ours. So we figured we had won the tryout, that we were on our way to Lyon.

We were very disappointed to learn that we came in second. The candidate from Chicago beat us. After I saw the judges' scoring sheet, I knew right away what had happened. The judge from Chicago had low-balled us and had high-balled the Chicago candidate. This made the difference between coming in first and coming in second. Although something this unprofessional should **never** happen, every so often it does happen. However, I don't give up easily. I thought, *If I'm not in Lyon in 1997, I'll definitely be there sometime in the near future."* But that is another story.

Dark Chocoloate Terrine
Yields 12 Portions

Ingredients

For the Chocolate Terrine:
10 ⅓ oz 56% Dark Chocolate
4 ¼ oz Unsalted Butter
2 each Egg Whites
1 ½ oz Sugar
8 oz Heavy Cream
7 each Egg Yolks, room temperature
1 ½ oz Sugar

For the Chocolate Glaze for Terrine:
1 ½ lb 56% Dark Chocolate
¾ oz Butter
1 pint Heavy Cream

Method

1. For the terrine, line a terrine mold with plastic wrap.
2. Combine the chocolate and butter together in a bowl. Put the bowl on top of a pot filled with a small amount of simmering water. Melt the chocolate and butter in the bowl over the hot water.
3. Beat the egg whites with 1 ½ oz of sugar until medium stiff. Remove from the bowl and reserve.
4. Beat the heavy cream until medium stiff. Remove from the bowl and reserve.
5. Place the egg yolks and 1 ½ oz of sugar in the mixing bowl and beat to ribbon stage.
6. Fold in the beaten egg whites in two stages. Mix well.
7. Fold in the whipped heavy cream in two stages. Mix well.
8. Pour the mixture into the terrine mold and set in the freezer. It will take about 4 hours to get solid frozen.
9. Cover the terrine with the chocolate glaze and put back in the freeze to set up.
10. Demold the chocolate terrine and put it on a glazing rack with the chocolate covered side of terrine face-down. Return to the freezer for a few minutes.
11. Remove the chocolate terrine from the freezer and pour the chocolate glaze over the entire terrine. Shake the terrine a little so the glaze distributes itself evenly. Put back in the freezer for a few minutes.
12. The terrine is now ready to use or can be wrapped in plastic wrap and kept in the freezer for several weeks.
13. For the glaze, finely chop the chocolate or use chocolate chips.
14. Over a water bath, melt the chocolate and butter on low heat.
15. In a sauce pan heat the cream – do not let it boil.
16. Add 1/3 of the cream to the chocolate and mix well.
17. Continue to add the cream by thirds until fully incorporated.

The Greenbrier Chevre Soufflé

Yields 2½ qt soufflé dish or 12 six-oz soufflé dishes

Ingredients

4 oz Unsalted Butter
¾ cup All-purpose Flour
2 cups Milk
6 oz Fresh Chèvre Cheese, broken up in pieces
6 each Egg Yolks
1 teaspoon Dried Thyme
to taste Kosher Salt
to taste Freshly Ground Black Pepper
8 each Egg White
½ teaspoon Dried Thyme

Method

1. Preheat the oven to 400F. Butter the inside of the soufflé dish or dishes. In a sauce pot melt the butter and then add the flour, making a roux, and cook for 2 - 3 minutes. Add the milk, whisking vigorously until the mixture is smooth and thick. Cook the mixture for another 2-3 minutes, stirring constantly to prevent it from burning on the bottom.

2. Remove the mixture from the stove and fold in the chèvre. Stir until the chèvre is melted and well incorporated. Stir in the egg yolks, one at the time. Add the salt, pepper and 1 teaspoon dried thyme.

3. With a Kitchen Aid, whip the egg whites to a soft peak. Fold ¼ of the whipped egg white into the cheese mixture to lighten it. Then carefully fold in the remaining egg white. Fill the prepared mixture into the soufflé molds, they should be about ¾ full. Sprinkle the top of the mixture with the ½ teaspoon dried thyme. Bake in the preheated oven until the top of the soufflés are golden brown and barely firm in the center. The large soufflé should take about 40-45 minutes, the small soufflés should take about 20-25 minutes. Serve immediately when the soufflés come out of the oven.

Cornish Game Hen Mediterranean
Herbed Orzo and Couscous, Tiny Green Beans and Red Bell Pepper Julienne
Yields 12 Portions

Ingredients

For the Cornish Game Hen:
¾ cup Olive Oil
2 Tbsp Finely Chopped Shallots
2 Tbsp Finely Chopped Garlic
6 oz Small White Mushrooms, quartered
6 oz Red Bell Peppers, cut in large julienne
6 oz Yellow Bell Peppers, cut in large julienne
6 oz Green Bell Peppers, cut in large julienne
6 oz Summer Squash, cut in large julienne
6 oz Carrots, cut in large julienne
3 oz Green Onion, split in half and cut two inches long
to taste Salt
to taste Freshly Ground Black Pepper
12 each Cornish Game Hen, 16 - 18 oz, completely boneless except for leg bones
3 Tbsp Finely Chopped Fresh Thyme
3 Tbsp Finely Chopped Fresh Rosemary
3 Tbsp Finely Chopped Fresh Oregano

For the orzo and couscous:
9 oz Orzo
5 oz Couscous
1 pint Chicken Stock
3 Tbsp oil
2 oz Macadamia Nuts, roasted and roughly chopped
2 Tbsp Fresh Chives, short cut
½ Tbsp Fresh Rosemary, chopped
1 ½ Tbsp Fresh Oregano, chopped
to taste Salt
to taste Freshly Ground Black Pepper

For the beans and red bell pepper:
12 oz French Beans, both ends trimmed off, cut in half and cooked
1 each Red Bell Pepper, cut in julienne and blanched
2 Tbsp Olive Oil
to taste Salt
to taste Freshly Ground Black Pepper

Cornish Game Hen Mediterranean
Herbed Orzo and Couscous, Tiny Green Beans and Red Bell Pepper Julienne

Method

1. For the Hen, place the first 12 items in a large bowl and toss well to combine.
2. Spread the vegetables on a large sheet pan and put in a 420F preheated oven.
3. Roast the vegetables until they are slightly caramelized and almost done. Remove from the oven and chill.
4. Form the vegetables into 12 balls using an ice cream scoop. Place these balls on a sheet pan and put in the freezer.
5. Spread the boneless Cornish game hens out on the table, skin side down. In the middle of each Cornish game hen place one vegetable ball and then wrap the Cornish game hen around it.
6. Turn the Cornish game hen over, skin side up and place on a sheet pan. Brush with butter and season with a little salt.
7. Roast at 380F for 25 minutes. Remove from the oven and keep warm.
8. For the orzo and couscous, cook the orzo in salted water until al dente, rinse with cold water and strain; reserve.
9. Cook the couscous in chicken stock until done, then strain through a chinoise. Spread on a plate and cool. Before serving, reheat with olive oil, nuts and herbs; keep hot.
10. For the beans and red bell pepper, heat the vegetables with olive oil in a skillet. Season with salt and pepper.
11. For plating, cut the Cornish game hens on a bias toward the head two times and set in the middle of the plate, showing the stuffing. On one side of the bird place the orzo couscous and on the other side the vegetables. In front of the bird drizzle a little poultry jus, which you can prepare from the bones.

Shellfish and Rice Bouillabaise Style
Yields 6 Portions

Ingredients

2 oz Olive Oil
½ oz Fresh Ginger, minced
½ oz Fresh Garlic, minced
½ oz Jalapeno, finely diced
3 oz Carrots, cut in ¼" squares
3 oz Leeks, cut in ¼" squares
3 oz Red Onions, cut in short julienne
3 oz Red Bell Pepper, cut in short julienne
3 qt Bouillabaisse Stock (prepared with commercial bouillabaisse base)
6 oz White Long Grain Rice, 10 minutes precooked
12 each P.E.I. Mussels
12 each East Coast Oysters
12 each 16/20 count IQF Shrimp, peeled & deveined
12 each 10/20 count Sea Scallops
4 oz Roma Tomatoes, peeled, seeded and diced
1 Tbsp Short-cut Chives
1 Tbsp Chopped Parsley
1 tsp Snipped-short Dill

Method

1. Sauté the ginger, garlic and jalapeno for a few minutes in the olive oil.
2. Add the vegetables and keep sautéing for two more minutes.
3. Add the bouillabaisse stock and bring to a simmer, cook until the vegetables are almost done.
4. Add the rice. When the rice is almost done, add the seafood and tomatoes. Leave on the heat for two more minutes.
5. Add herbs and serve immediately.

Bocuse d'Or

By 8am, the bleachers were packed with spectators from 12 different countries.

In 1999, during the NRA show in Chicago, I was selected to be on the jury to choose the U.S. candidate for the Bocuse d'Or in 2001. Judging can really give you a competitive edge. Judging this event was particularly beneficial as it gave me some insight into what judges were looking for in a Bocuse d'Or candidate, and I fully intended to try out again in the future. I listened carefully, learned a lot and took copious notes.

Then in 2000, when the 2003 Bocuse d'Or tryouts took place in Chicago, I was a competitor. I did not have enough time to find an apprentice, who would be eligible for the no-more-than-22-years-old requirement three years later, but I was very impressed with Kate Morrissey who worked part time for me at the restaurant. This Hocking College student had the right attitude and a solid work ethic. Not only was she the right age to be my apprentice for the tryout, but she also agreed to participate.

The main protein ingredients for this particular competition were duck and striped bass. We had to prepare a twelve-portion platter for each protein. Any extra protein and accompaniments on the tray were our choice. For several months, we did some intensive practice sessions. In the third week of May 2000, we traveled to Chicago. Kate was a little nervous to perform in front of the large audience there, but she did an outstanding job. We did have one small hiccup during plating.

We were using a fondant gun to place the sauce on our duck platter. Kate held the gun as I poured the sauce into the top of it. Neither of us realized, however, that the outlet on the bottom was not completely closed. Fortune was with us in that moment, for the tip of the gun was aimed at the table and the platter remained pristine. We lost some sauce, but still had enough for the platter and the gravy boat. This was actually the only critical moment of the competition; otherwise, everything went very smoothly.

I had to build a team that would support me in every aspect. Michel Bouit would take care all of all the logistics. To secure financial funding for this undertaking, we established the American Bocuse d'Or Culinary Institute, spearheaded by Harry Henning, a lawyer from Porter Wright, and Jim Budros, a financial advisor with Budros, Ruhlin and Roe. Our budget was set at $150,000. I also had to find an appropriately-young apprentice, who was excited to work with food, willing to work long hours and willing to go the extra mile. Lastly, I needed a coach, preferably a French chef with Bocuse d'Or experience.

Obviously, raising $150,000 was not an easy task. While until now I had financed all competitions on my own, the amount for the Bocuse d'Or was more than I could handle. Harry, Jim and I made plans to raise funds. Several times we sent more than 400 letters to potential donors, asking them for their support. We approached restaurant suppliers, we held fundraising cocktail parties and dinners, and we sold memorabilia plates that Villeroy and Boch produced for us.

For the competition, all candidates were required to have a poster. I found a student from the Columbus College of Art & Design, who designed and created the poster - a painting of me at the Bocuse d'Or. We listed our major sponsors on the poster, printed several hundred and sold them. Of course, I autographed the plates and posters - to increase their value.

Through our fundraising efforts, we found two main sponsors: Electrolux and OSO Sweet Onions from South America. Each gave us $15,000. Although none of our other corporate sponsors gave quite as much as Electrolux and OSO Sweet Onions, every dollar helped us reach our goal. The support we received from the Columbus community was tremendous. *The Dispatch* ran a series of helpful articles about our Bocuse d'Or project and our progress. Mr. John Wolfe, the publisher of *The Dispatch*, assigned his food writer, Robin Davis, to our project. During the final week of practice, Ms. Davis spent an entire night with us at a practice session. Then she traveled with us to Lyon!

During the 2001 Bocuse d'Or competition, Michel recommended that I travel to France to experience the competition firsthand. What I saw there was simply unbelievable. On the main floor of the event, 12 identical kitchens were set up, each with the chef's name and country printed on a big sign overhead. Two long judging tables with 12 chairs each were set up in front of the kitchens. Each participating country provided one judge. Twelve judges critiqued the fish platters and the other 12 judged the meat platters. Opposite the kitchens were spectator bleachers - with seating for a couple thousand people. Once the competition started, these bleachers were packed with fans from the chefs' home countries waving flags and banners, beating drums, playing other musical instruments and screaming. The noise level was mind-boggling. The electric atmosphere reminded me of the crowd in a soccer stadium. It was a great learning experience for me, for I now knew what to expect in 2003.

Following the competition, we stayed in France a few more days. Michel had organized a little tour for our group of 17 travelers. We stayed in some beautiful *chateaus* and consumed some great dinners. One such dinner took place in a private home with truffles served at every course. What a treat!

One afternoon, we even went truffle hunting - first with a dog and later with a pig. When the dog indicated the right spot where we would find the truffle, he received a piece of cheese as a treat. With the pig, it was a completely different story. As soon as the pig found a truffle location, it started digging. Then you had to pull the pig away - otherwise the truffle would be gone. Pigs love truffles!

We also visited a truffle "market." The buying and selling of truffles took place in the back room of a restaurant or out of the trunk of a car. Everything was top secret. Nick, who made a documentary about truffles, was permitted to film the "wheelers and dealers", who always covered up the license plates of their cars. Apparently they didn't want to pay the sales tax.

After returning to Columbus, I started looking for an apprentice for 2003 in Lyon. I contacted a few of my friends at the CIA to help me search for the right individual. After a few months, we had a list of students who were interested in participating. I went to the CIA to interview them. The results were not very encouraging. Although they were all very good students with excellent grades, when I inquired about their motivation for participating in the Bocuse d'Or, most of them responded that they thought they might be famous if we did well. Hardly anyone mentioned that it would be a great learning experience for them. Eventually I found a young man who I thought might meet my criteria. He was ready to start his externship, but hadn't yet committed himself to a restaurant. I suggested he do his externship at Handke's Cuisine, which would provide me a chance for further evaluation. However, at the end of his externship, I just didn't feel he was quite the right person. So, he completed his externship at Handke's Cuisine, but was no longer my Bocuse d'Or apprentice.

In the meantime, Michel had made arrangements for me to do a practice session at a culinary school in Paris. During this trip, I met the chef at the Ritz in Paris, Michel Roth, the 1991 Bocuse d'Or winner. After he served us a fabulous truffle dinner, he gave us a tour of the absolutely gorgeous kitchen - painted tiles floor to ceiling, lots of polished copper pots and pans and a stainless steel ceiling. Michel had also contacted French master chef Bernard Leprince, who had coached the 2001 French chef, Francois Adamski, to the top of the podium. Chef Leprince was interested in working with me. We made a contract with him, and Chef Leprince came on board as my coach in the summer of 2002. He traveled to Columbus every month for two or three days until November, and we developed our game plan.

Michel also contacted a silversmith in France, who had previously produced platters for Bocuse d'Or competitors. There were some new rules that year for the platter's size: its dimensions could not exceed one meter by one meter. Naturally, the platters also had to have a special design. After several proposals, we reached an agreement and ordered our two platters. Each platter cost about $15,000.

Around February 2002, my friends at the CIA selected another apprentice candidate for me. I was very pleased: this one met my criteria. Heather Brinker was a 19-year-old CIA student originally from Baraboo, Wisconsin. She was ready to begin her externship from the middle of March to the middle of July. If Heather would prove to be my apprentice, she would take a leave of absence from the school until after the competition, then return to school and graduate. It didn't take long for me to know that she was just the right person. She was hard working, passionate about food, teachable and willing to go the extra mile. It would be great to have her on the team. Heather, her parents and the school administrators agreed to my proposal. In July, I had an apprentice and a coach. We were ready to go.

My coach, Bernard, came to Columbus for the first time in the middle of July and we started working on accompaniments and garnishes. I would work on the required protein - Norwegian sea trout for the fish platter and oxtail and beef tenderloin for the meat platter - between his visits. The tenderloin was relatively easy to work with. The oxtail was a different story. To bone a raw oxtail is challenging, so I braised the whole tail, removed the meat from the bone, and attempted to put the meat back into an oxtail shape. It just would not hold together even when I tried using meat glue. So I had no choice but to bone the raw tail. At first, this took me a long time., But after I boned about 120 tails, I got pretty efficient. Eventually, I could bone an oxtail in about five minutes! After boning two tails, I placed the meat side by side (touching) and began to reconstruct the oxtail. First, I wrapped bleached leaks around a pre-cooked carrot. Then, I wrapped a sheet of slightly frozen veal forcemeat around the leaks. Finally, I covered everything with the oxtail meat. I wrapped the whole bundle in a cheese cloth, tied it with butcher twine, and braised it the traditional way. For the beef tenderloin, we reversed things. We put the meat *inside,* wrapped it in veal forcemeat, and finally wrapped it in a sheet of thinly sliced mushrooms. It was actually a beef tenderloin *crepinette.*

During our practice sessions over the next several months, we cooked a lot of beef tenderloin and oxtails. So, we had to find a good use for all of the meat. Since the chefs at Handke's Cuisine had a family-style meal every day at 3pm, we served it there. After a while, my chefs asked if they could have chicken occasionally. During the months that I was practicing, they ate beef tenderloin almost every other day.

The Norwegian sea trout was shipped to us whenever we needed it and we developed a nice concept with this fish as well. Heather and I spent many hours in the kitchen, practicing to improve quality and speed and developing new accompaniments.

In October 2002, I decided to take Heather to Lyon to get her used to the new environment. I planned for us to prepare both dishes in the small banquet kitchen of the hotel outside of Lyon, where we would stay in January during the competition. Nick Versteeg came with us. He was working on the documentary called "The Bocuse d'Or: A Chef's Dream" about the 2003 Bocuse d'Or for the food channel, focusing on the Canadian, Icelandic, French and American (me) candidates. Nick had already been in Columbus several times before during our practice sessions. Michel, with his wife, Liz, came along as coordinator and translator. He had asked some French chefs to see and critique our work. Bernard met us in Lyon, and - to my surprise - he brought along a female food writer, who worked for a French food magazine. That was not my idea at all! When she started taking pictures, I ordered her to leave. Overall, we had a good practice session with good, constructive feedback from the French chefs. Heather took copious notes and kept a detailed log of preparation times.

During this trip, we also visited Paul Bocuse's original restaurant, l'Auberge du Pont de Collonges. Outside the restaurant, there is an area where bronze plaques with all of the Bocuse d'Or winners' names carved into them are laid into the floor at a reception immediately following the competition. Heather and I promised ourselves that our names would be there in 2003.

We returned to Columbus, and continued to change and improve our platters. However when December - the busiest month at the restaurant - arrived, we had to put our competition project on the back burner. During this season, our focus was to earn money and please clients. When the Christmas holidays and New Year celebrations were behind us, we only had three and a half weeks until we would cook in Lyon.

From January 3 on, every other night Heather and I cooked the entire program for Lyon. The restaurant closed each night at 10pm and then the chefs cleaned the kitchen. After this, at around 11pm, Heather and I set up our ingredients, cooked for five and a half hours and cleaned the kitchen again. Then I drove Heather home (she lived in German Village) and I drove home to Dublin. I slept a few hours, shopped at 9am and was back at the restaurant by 10am. Heather came to work at 2pm. We repeated that schedule every other day. We completed ten full sessions before our departure to Lyon. After four sessions, I asked one of our young culinarians, John, if he would be willing to stay with us through the night to help clean up. He agreed and as a bonus I took him to Lyon, where he was helpful to us as well.

On the day we left Columbus, Margot, Heather, John and I each filled our two suitcases with all our equipment - pots, pans, bowls, knives, a food processor, an electric voltage convertor, uniforms and some personal items. Naturally, we had to open our suitcases for TSA to check everything. I had three stainless steels bowls nested tightly together in my suitcase. When I tried to separate them, I broke the tip of my left index finger. Although it hurt a little, we couldn't do anything about it.

The next day around noon, we arrived in Lyon. We settled into our hotel outside of Lyon and got organized. In the evening, there was a dinner reception at the banquet facility of our hotel for all of our American fans. Heather and I stood by the door to welcome everyone, shake their hands, and receive well wishes. Michel had a group of 165 people - the largest ever contingent from the U.S.A. for a Bocuse d'Or competition. The next day we went shopping, did some *mise en place*, or preparations, for one more practice session with the local ingredients.

The World Pastry Cup takes place in Lyon just before the Bocuse d'Or competition. There is also a restaurant and hotel trade show running simultaneously during both competitions. The owner of our hotel was a member of the organizing committee. We were surprised to learn, that he had planned a party every evening in the bar downstairs that lasted until five or six in the morning. His guests smoked cigars and cigarettes like crazy, and the smoke rose all the way to our room on the third floor. One morning, I counted 60 empty champagne cases. Despite the parties, the next few days went by very quickly.

Monday afternoon was the official opening of the Bocuse d'Or competition with a group photo and speeches. Tuesday morning, the first 12 candidates cooked. Heather and I were scheduled for the second day, Wednesday. On Tuesday, Heather and I continued to prepare. We woke up on Wednesday at 4am, had some oatmeal for breakfast and then loaded everything onto our bus. Michel had arranged the logistics very well. For example, when we arrived at the competition venue, our bus could drive right up to the back door of the hall, which made unloading very easy for us. We organized our kitchen. Competing in the slot just ahead of us was Chef Franck Putelat from France. Opposite us on the bleachers, Michel had reserved seats for our fans, who all wore long-sleeved Team Handke t-shirts with the U.S.

flag, the Bocuse d'Or logo, Electrolux, OSO Sweet Onion and Handke's Cuisine printed on them. They waved Handke's Cuisine towels. By 8am, the bleachers were packed with spectators from 12 different countries. The noise was unbelievable, and communication between Heather and me was limited to sign language even though we were working side by side. Nick attached microphones to Heather, me and some jury members - to make the documentary more real. The kitchen proctors inspected our ingredients, and we started cooking around 9am with five and a half hours of stressful work ahead of us.

Heather and I each had a to-do list, that I had prepared, which was very helpful. We both knew exactly what our tasks were. When our time came to plate, we were ready. What we did not know was that Chef Franck was late. Under normal circumstances, a late competitor would be disqualified or would be instructed to present his platter after the last competitor was done - some two hours later. In this case, however, the rules were bent: they made us wait more than five minutes with our fish platter. In those minutes our fish became overdone. I did not overcook it; it was overdone from just sitting there. Our meat platter, however, was perfect. Now we just had to wait another three hours for the results.

All the competitors marched in with their countries' flags. First they announced the best fish platter - Belgium. Then they announced the best meat platter - U.S.A. At this point, I knew already that we would not make the podium. Heather, on the other hand, did not realize this, and she was very excited. When the podium winners were announced and our names were not called, she was shocked - and she broke down. For the last nine months, she had worked very hard, given all she had, postponed her graduation and sacrificed her personal life. I really felt sorry for her... and also so very proud of her. I was very disappointed as well. Coming into the competition, I really thought we would make the podium. Out of a possible 1,000 points, we came in sixth - with just 40 points less than the winner. To compare this with the 2001 competition, the difference between first and second place was 200 points. Until the last year, 2015, we were the best U.S.A. Bocuse d'Or finisher since its inception in 1985.

Today, when I look at the photographs of Chef Franck's platters and ours, I wonder how they were so similar. Being my own fundraiser, travel agent, marketing person and cook, (and maybe the oldest Bocuse d'Or competitor ever), I must say - and I think I can speak for Heather as well - it was a great learning experience with a lot of excitement. I never could have done it without the support of my wife, Margot, my daughters, Heather, my friends and all of the people who supported me in this endeavor.

A recipe full of spices and fond memories of Bocuse d'Or is ***Original Texas Chili***.

Original Texas Chili for Bocuse d'Or
Yields 12 Portions

Ingredients

2 oz Dried Ancho Chili Peppers
1 cup Water
3 oz Vegetable Oil
2 lb Lean Beef Chuck, Beef Strip Loin or Beef Tenderloin, cut into ¼-inch pieces
2 cups Black Beans, pre-soaked
3 cups Beef Stock
2 oz Garlic, fine chopped
¾ cup Yellow Onion, small diced
2 Tbsp Cumin, ground
1 Tbsp Oregano, ground
½ cup Paprika
to taste Salt
1/3 cup Jalapeño, fine diced
2 Tbsp Cilantro, chopped
1 tsp Sour Cream
Cilantro Plushes

Method

1. Remove the seeds and stems from the ancho chili peppers and place in a sauce pot. Cover with water and bring to a boil. Remove from the heat, cover and let stand for 15 minutes. Purée the chilies in a blender with the cooking liquid until smooth; reserve.
2. In a large frying pan over high heat, add the vegetable oil and brown the meat. You might have to do this in three or four batches, otherwise the meat starts "boiling" and get's tough.
3. Transfer the meat to a heavy-bottomed sauce pot. Add the pureed chilies, black beans and beef stock. Make sure you have enough liquid to cover the meat and the beans. Simmer for 30 minutes.
4. Add the garlic, onions, cumin, oregano, paprika, jalapeño and salt. Simmer until the meat and beans are tender.
5. Add the chopped cilantro and serve in soup bowls. Garnish with sour cream and cilantro plushes.

Handke's Cuisine

The FBI and their big, bomb-sniffing dogs searched the entire van!

Now we'll hop back to my career. On June 1, 1991, we left White Sulphur Springs to move back to Columbus, Ohio. Then we bought a house, bought a business and opened a restaurant called Pete's Steakhouse - all in just three weeks! The previous restaurant proprietor left on a Saturday. We took inventory on Sunday and opened on Monday, June 21, 1991. We operated as Pete's Steakhouse until August, when we changed the name to Handke's Cuisine. Our very own place.

Owning a business in the United States was a completely new experience for us. The furniture and some of the kitchen equipment belonged to the Edwards Company and was supplied to us as part of the lease. We had to purchase everything else from the previous restaurant proprietors: the wine and food inventory, the computer system and some of the kitchen equipment. It took EVERYTHING we had saved. Unfortunately, the outdated computer system didn't work for us. Sometimes if you're too anxious for something, you don't pay enough attention to the details. I had hurried because I didn't want to miss an opportunity. I confess now, if I would have listened to my wife, I would have avoided this stress and maybe saved some money as well.

When we took over the business, we also took over the staff. For the first couple of weeks, we even used *Pete's Steakhouse* menu. We had 10,000 square feet with160 seats downstairs and 70 seats upstairs in the bar. We were leasing the space for a pretty penny. And business was off to a very slow start.

As luck would have it, I soon met Ian Rodier, JD, who helped us restructure our lease a little, since we were spending more than we were earning. Ian talked to Mr. Edwards, who agreed to the new terms. To this day, I am very grateful for the advice Ian gave us.

In the very beginning we served lunch and dinner both upstairs and downstairs. However, the waiters did not like working upstairs, because they had to walk up and down the staircase. Furthermore, although we had a dumb waiter to deliver food upstairs, the wait staff sometimes forgot to take the food out of it. We stopped serving dinner upstairs fairly quickly. After two years, we stopped serving lunch upstairs as well. The business crowd preferred the more intimate, vaulted ceilinged, wine-cellar-like downstairs setting for lunch. Eventually, we stopped serving lunch completely to focus on dinner and catering.

Within six months, we had changed and replaced almost everything - including the staff. We needed a fresh start. One thing I had really counted on was my former Athletic Club clientele following me, but that did not happen. Once in a while a member from the Athletic Club would say, "Oh, I didn't know you were here." Maybe I had been away too long. In any case, we had to build a completely new clientele.

We also counted on newspaper food critics to "advertise" for us. However, a business editor from *The Dispatch* wrote the first article about our restaurant. This move so upset *The Dispatch's* food critic, The Grumpy Gourmet, who had wanted to write the article, that he waited nine more months to write about us. When "the Grump" finally came to the restaurant, he walked down the stairs and asked Margot, who was at the front desk, if the "fry cook" was in. Margot informed him right away that the chef was not a "fry cook," but a rather a CMC. That broke the ice, and we became good friends. He respected our business. Over the years, he did a lot of good for us with his articles in the newspaper. He's been retired for quite a few years. But every once in a while, I call him for his well-informed restaurant news and gossip. Two or three times a year, I take him head cheese, pea soup with ham hocks, chili and gumbo - his favorite comfort foods. Once I cooked him a brined veal tongue, which he didn't care for and he gave to the neighbors. What I really admire about the Grump is he never expects handouts. He always paid for everything he consumed at the restaurant. He wouldn't even accept a chocolate-dipped strawberry on the house. Sometimes food critics actually expect free food, which, while not the way it should be, is the way it is. While Grump's first review of Handke's was glowing, he ranked us very expensive, which can scare away the general public.

1991 was a difficult year to start a business anyway because the country was in a recession. In the late summer and early fall, we had plenty of parties booked for Christmas. However, when the recession started on the East Coast, many of our previously-booked Christmas parties were canceled.

In addition to the recession, I also miscalculated New Year's Eve business. In Europe, the New Year's Eve celebration is huge. Although I bought five or six cases of champagne, we only sold three bottles! I should've known that Americans don't celebrate the way we do in Europe, but I guess I got excited. By shortly after midnight, all of our customers had gone home. Europeans, on the other hand, celebrate until the wee hours. In later years, I gave a free glass of champagne to anyone who stayed late.

The first year at Handke's Cuisine business was so bad that I was ready to throw in the towel. Since I knew some key people at the Broadmoor Hotel in Colorado Springs from my days at The Greenbrier, I tried for a chef position there. The Broadmoor, however, was acquired by the Gaylords, who also already owned the Opryland Hotel in Nashville. The former chef from the Opryland Hotel was also looking for a job since his own restaurant venture hadn't fared too well. Since the two executives at the Broadmoor had worked with this chef from his days at the Opryland Hotel, they hired him. Since I didn't get the job, we hung on in Columbus at Handke's Cuisine.

Given our difficult times, I brought some equipment from home - like my own Cuisinart - because I couldn't afford to buy a new one for the restaurant. After a while, when business got better, we established credit with our suppliers. This situation allowed us to get delivery all month long, with one combined statement at the end of the month or the beginning of the next one. The companies then gave us two weeks to pay. On the thirteenth of the month, I received all of the checks from our bookkeeper, signed and mailed. Everyone had their money on the 15th. I was very proud to say that I owed nobody a penny in this town.

However, we had a problem in the very beginning with one of our suppliers. We fell a little bit behind with our produce supplier, who I had used at the Athletic Club for eight years. After two months, he started bugging me for his money. He called daily, saying, "I really need my money." I told him, "Don't worry, but right now it's a little bit tight." Finally I had the money and I told him to come get the check. He said, "I knew you would pay." However, when he came to get his check, I "divorced" him. I never bought another head of lettuce from him. When we were well established, he sent his son and his salesperson to the restaurant to court my business. Even at his tailgate parties, he offered me things, and I just wouldn't accept. Forgiven, but not forgotten. Does that make me a bad guy?

For a while I got all of my seafood from Boston, my mushrooms from the West Coast and foie gras from the Hudson Valley. I still not only do business, but also have credit accounts with all of these suppliers. We paid our vendors by check; we did not use credit cards at all.

We are very grateful for Mr. Edwards' genuine support of our business. We met weekly with him. He provided us with feedback from our customers, who were his friends. He allowed us to make copies in his office for free. He did mailings for us -

newsletters, marketing pieces and advertising to drum up business. At one point, he sent an introduction letter for Handke's Cuisine to members of the Columbus Country Club, the Scioto Country Club and the Athletic Club of Columbus for us. When he was running Pete's Steakhouse, he had mailed out a lot of coupons. He instructed us to accept those coupons, and he personally reimbursed us for them.

Mr. Edwards loved my *Crème Brûlèe*. He used to come for dinner and order six crème brûlèes. Then he strolled around the restaurant, handing out the luscious dessert to happy diners. One day he said to me, "You should visit local hotels and take them crème brûlèe. Leave free samples at the front desk." That started a marketing campaign that we carried out for 17 years. Every three weeks, I prepared 120 crème brûlèes in two-ounce foil cups. I placed each dessert on a six-inch plate with a plastic spoon, a chocolate-dipped strawberry, a beverage napkin that advertised Handke's Cuisine and a business card. At hotels downtown, near the airport and in the Easton area, I left treats for bellhops, concierges, receptionists and anyone who looked like they might be willing to tell a guest about Handke's Cuisine. I thanked them for sending customers to my restaurant. I handed out menus as well. It was cheaper and more effective than any ad in a magazine or newspaper.

I also got some free television "advertising" through cooking demonstrations at an affiliate station of Channel 10 in Grandview. For example, they once asked me to do a three-minute segment on what to do with Thanksgiving turkey leftovers. When I arrived at the station Friday morning at 7am, they told me that I only had two minutes (instead of the promised three). I also sometimes did cooking demonstrations on Channel 4 and Channel 6. More free advertising. But all were very short. I had to be well prepared and talk fast.

Around 1994, a friend and certified master chef in Grand Rapids, Michigan suggested my name for an ad campaign for the *Meijer* store chain. They wanted to film a 30-second segment in the restaurant with me and my Culinary Olympic medals. I had one line: "That's why I buy my fruits and vegetables at Meijer." It took about 15 cuts to get my part right because I kept saying "Meijer's" instead of "Meijer." They paid me $500. But the commercial ran for more than six months on channels 4, 6 and 10 many times every day. I was also on billboards in town. Everyone knew me.

From then on, I spent about $100,000 at Meijer annually, buying produce by the case. Every morning I left the house at 6:30am and went straight to Meijer. I had nice relationships with the store employees. Sometimes they even opened up a check-out counter for me, so I did not have to wait. If I forget something, I called the store and Margot would pick things up for me at 1pm on her way to work. They told her, if I didn't like the product, I could return it the next morning.

Every year Meijer holds a big corporate meeting in Grand Rapids, Michigan for all the vendors. Mr. Meijer had a botanical garden there, and we were invited for dinner one evening in the garden. I found out his wife's family came from Germany in a town very near my hometown. They were very nice, down-to-earth people.

* * *

Susi had finished high school in Lewisburg. She was going to start her training at the CIA in September. She had some experience working at The Greenbrier during her vacation time. I also began taking apprentices again because I was familiar with the program from my time at the Athletic Club of Columbus. But, I was not aware that the situation had changed. It used to be that an apprentice had to stay in one place for his or her entire apprenticeship. If the restaurant could not fulfill certain curricular criteria, however, then the apprentice worked elsewhere for a period of time. So I took an apprentice. After one year, he came and said, "Chef, I need to talk to you. I think I've learned everything here that I can learn. I want to finish my apprenticeship at another restaurant." So I talked to the department head at Columbus State, and they sent me another. The same thing happened! After that, I stopped taking apprentices. Why should I train an apprentice for someone else? It takes about a year for an apprentice to be productive.

I devised an alternate plan instead. I had very good contacts with instructors at the CIA. My friends there handpicked some really good students, who needed to spend three or four months in an externship. They had already been in school for nine months, and they had a good amount of skills. This worked very well for us.

I taught cooking classes in Columbus with Betty Rosbottom, who was at Lazarus' restaurant, *La Belle Pomme*. Betty created menus, and taught her students how to prepare them with the help of Steve Stover, Jim Budros, Rich Terapak, me and others. Then she served her students little tastes. I agreed to teach since it didn't cost me anything.

After six months of teaching at *La Belle Pomme*, I decided to teach cooking classes at my restaurant. When Betty heard about it, she asked me to make it a wine dinner, so it would be distinctly unique from her courses. But I couldn't do that, since we weren't really pairing the wine that closely. Betty was pretty upset, and that was the end of my cooking classes at *La Belle Pomme*.

I taught cooking classes once a month to a maximum of 36 people at Handke's

Cuisine. My class drew housewives, secretaries, divorcees, doctors and lawyers. We didn't have much technology yet, so we advertised the classes by newsletter. We attracted so many students that for a period of time we taught two classes, back to back, every month.

Another successful marketing tool was donating food for events. When the Columbus Academy, Columbus School for Girls and the Franklin Park Conservatory held their annual antique shows, they invited me to hand out appetizers like smoked salmon, crème brûlée, pâtés and seafood terrines. We provided the food at no cost, handed out menus and business cards and talked to the attendees, who happened to be our targeted clientele. I found this strategy most effective when I attended myself. Also, several times a year, organizations like the Columbus Symphony and the Rotary Club held silent auction fundraising events. For these, we donated multi-course dinners, which I would prepare in the homes of the highest bidders - for eight to ten people.

Eventually, after we discontinued lunch in 1993 and focused on dinner and off-premise catering, things at Handke's Cuisine improved. In 1992, we also decided to discontinue our valet parking service for which we had hired students, who were not terribly reliable, given their class schedule. Sometimes they didn't show up at all. More than once, I had to park cars. On one particularly bad evening, the car of OSU's former president, Mr. Jennings, was stolen. It was a never-ending drama. Finally, we contracted with Parking Solutions, a valet company started by Aaron Shocket, who did an excellent job for us. Since we were one of his first customers, Mr. Shocket never raised our fees and Mr. Edwards allowed us to use the garage on Blenkner Street free of charge. We used them until the restaurant closed.

Eventually, we also outsourced the wait staff for event catering. It is especially difficult to get wait staff around the holidays. Often, you had to take whomever came through the door. Finding good wait staff for the restaurant was a little easier. However, the problem here in the U.S. is that a waiter is not a professional. In Germany a waiter has to complete a three-year apprenticeship to become a server. In the United States, if you can carry two plates, you're a server. The position is viewed as a job - not a profession.

In 1992, my friend David Kellaway was the executive chef at Salish Lodge and Spa at Snoqualmie Falls outside of Seattle. He decided to stage a CMC dinner. Because he had completed his CMC test just a few years before, he thought it was a great idea to promote certified master chef status with a dinner. So he invited me and four other CMCs and one CMPC, Chris Northmore, to prepare the meal. The hotel paid for our airfare, lodging and ingredients. Each of us had to prepare one course for the meal. The hotel's sommelier paired the appropriate wines. The dinner was planned for a Friday night, so we all arrived on Wednesday. David picked us up at the airport, and it was like a reunion since we hadn't seen each other for a while. Thursday morning we went to Pike Place Market in Seattle to see what was available, shop and then plan our menu accordingly. Pike Place Market is a paradise for a chef! It's unbelievable how the vendors display their merchandise and incredible what you can buy there. Dinner for our 90 guests on Friday was a complete success. After this experience, I made a decision right away: I would do this at Handke's Cuisine.

In January 1993, we held the first CMC dinner in Columbus. For the next few years we held CMC dinners in either January or February, until we eventually found that the first Monday in March was ideal. I believe our CMC dinners were the finest dinners ever served in Columbus. On the evening of the dinner, guests already made their reservations for the following year. Every year we were fully booked with 140 attendees. From 1993 - 2008, 35 different CMCs came to Handke's Cuisine to support me, which I really appreciated. I have wonderful memories of these times. 2001 was a particularly special year. I was able to get the 1988 U.S. and German National Culinary Olympic teams to come for the International CMC Collaboration Dinner. We continued these special dinners until we sold our business in 2008.

Over the years, some other CMCs got on the dinner bandwagon as well. I participated in these events in Atlanta, Detroit, Houston and just outside of Baltimore - at my friend Rudy Speckamp's place, *Rudy's 2900*.

During the middle 1990s, I also taught one-week continuing education courses at the CIA with topics like *garde manger*, food show competitions, cold buffet and *a la carte* presentations. At one of these classes, I met a chef from Santiago, Chile - René Acklin, who was originally from Switzerland but had lived in Santiago for many years. He was visiting his daughter, a student at the CIA. Since he was also interested in brushing up on culinary knowledge, he enrolled in my food show course while he was there. We then became very good friends. He asked the CIA to send me to Santiago to teach some classes to executive chefs at Fundación Chile, which was a food research institute. The CIA agreed and in 1993 I taught the first course there - international cuisine. The last day of the curriculum was supposed to be South American, but since that's where we were, I changed it to U.S. cuisine, with Cornish game hen as the main ingredient. When you stuff poultry, like Cornish Game Hen, it's best to pre-cook the filling. That way, the bird doesn't dry out waiting for the stuffing to cook, but rather it remains tender and juicy.

Since I don't speak Spanish, I had to work with an interpreter. Therefore, instead of being done at 2pm, my classes lasted until 5pm. But apparently they liked me, because I was invited back the following year to teach a Food Show Competition class. The week following this course, a pastry chef from the CIA was supposed to teach Plated Kitchen Desserts. However, the pastry chef got sick and couldn't travel. So the CIA asked me to stay a second week to teach the pastry class. Never afraid of a challenge, I accepted. You don't necessarily have to be a full-fledged pastry chef to prepare plated kitchen desserts - as long as you have some pastry background. I made it through the course - even though I had to consult with my pastry chef friend, Chris Northmore, in Atlanta several times. In South America, flour, butter, eggs and cream are different from North American ingredients, and sometimes you have to make adjustments to the recipes.

Every year in Santiago, there is a Restaurant and Motel Trade Show called *ExpoGourmand*. Two restaurants from the United States were invited to participate; the restaurants would send their executive chef or owner along with two or three other chefs to the show, where they would run one of two restaurants (one seated 110 guests and the other seated 130 guests). Chef René was part of the organizing committee. They selected Le Bernardin from New York City with Chef Eric Ripert and Handke's Cuisine from Columbus, Ohio. Wow - what an honor! I readily accepted the invitation.

My former *sous chef* from The Greenbrier, Scott Bennett, who had moved to Columbus as the executive chef at the Wedgewood Country Club, accepted my invitation to join my team in Santiago. A young lady, Touria Semingson, from Nelsonville, who worked for me at Handke's Cuisine and spoke a little Spanish, became the third member of the team. We also were provided with local help in Santiago. For this event, I created five, five-course menus, using a lot of local ingredients. Our restaurant was on the same floor as the kitchen and had room for 110 guests. Eric's restaurant was upstairs with 130 seats. The first night went very well, and we were booked for the next four days. Dinner service started around 9:30pm and when we left the kitchen at midnight, all of us - Le Bernardin and Handke's Cuisine went out together to sample the local cuisine. I liked the **Shrimp Quesadilla** so much that I developed my own recipe for it. We also enjoyed drinking **Pisco Sours**, a refreshing combination of confectioner's sugar, Chilean Pisco and lemon or lime juice.

In Santiago, Handke's Cuisine and Le Bernardin shared the same kitchen - Handke's Cuisine chefs were on one side and Le Bernardin's were on the other. On the second evening, Chef Eric came to the kitchen around 10:45, when they were ready to serve the main course, because they were about 15 portions of the entrée short, and there was no more food in the kitchen. His chefs had miscounted the entrées! What happened next was not very pretty; I won't go into details. But Chef Eric announced right then and there, "No, more going out to dinner until we are done with our project." Things settled down after a while, and it was, overall, a great experience for everybody.

Margot accompanied me on this trip since she hadn't been to Chile before. After the show, Margot and my two helpers returned to Columbus. At this time, I was also a member of the United Airlines Culinary Consulting Team with Victor Gielisse, so I stayed on in South America. I met up with my colleagues from United Airlines in Santiago for one day, then flew to Buenos Aires, for just one day, and then flew to Rio de Janiero, Brazil, for a major menu development session. I must have arrived in Rio sooner than I had outlined to Margot.

After I checked into the hotel, I explored the hotel lobby and spotted the jewelry store, H. Stern. In the showcase they had a beautiful rainbow gemstone necklace, and I thought it would be a wonderful gift for Margot. I ventured into the store where they showed the necklace to me. It was so beautiful! The price was steep, but I had already decided I would buy it - never mind the price. Naturally, I didn't have that much cash with me, but my credit card was accepted. I put the little box with the necklace in the safe in my room, and we all went out for dinner. I decided to pay for dinner this evening, which really didn't matter because I'd be reimbursed for our travel expenses anyway. But the waitress soon returned to the table: my credit card had been declined. She tried it again with the same results. As soon as I returned to the hotel, I called Margot to tell her what had happened. Earlier that day, she had received a call from American Express, who told her that someone in Rio had charged a large amount on our credit card, and - since I wasn't supposed to be there yet - she thought it was fraud and canceled the credit card. We straightened things out. Margot loved her new necklace.

As I mentioned above, from 1992-1997, I was a member of the United Airlines Culinary Consulting Team, which started when United Airlines took over the routes from Pan American, who had gone bankrupt. Victor Gielisse did some work for United, but since the workload was heavy, they invited me to join the team. Besides the two of us, the team consisted of the corporate executive chef for international flights, the corporate executive chef for domestic flights, menu design people, in-flight supervisors and regional managers. We had menu development sessions every so often for inbound and outbound United flights worldwide. We were mostly involved in first and business class meals. Although food was served also in coach/economy class, we didn't spend much time on it. United had large flight kitchens in places like New York, Chicago, Los Angeles, San Francisco, Honolulu, Seattle, Miami and Washington, DC - just to mention a few. Most of the time, we went to these places for two or three days and worked with the executive chefs of these locations. For two full days, we worked with staff, chosen by the executive chefs, to prepare recipes that we had developed for new menu items. On the third day, we displayed everything we had prepared on large tables and provided detailed descriptions to everyone mentioned above. While they generally liked what we produced, occasionally we had to slightly alter the recipe. Overall, we did very well.

After the first year, however, we discovered that we had a problem. We created all outbound and inbound recipes - for both international and domestic flights - from our home bases in the United States. Therefore, sometimes we developed an inbound meal recipe for Hong Kong that the chef in Hong Kong couldn't produce because he didn't have the same ingredients there that we were using in the United States. From then on, we developed all inbound meals on location in Tokyo, Hong Kong, Singapore, South America and Europe. During my five years consulting with United, we tasted all of kinds of different dishes in different countries and restaurants. The philosophy of United was the food should reflect what the customer would eat at his destination. For the customer returning to the United States, we always served a nice steak menu. United believed that after spending two weeks in Asia eating sushi, rice, chow mein and Peking duck, the customer was ready for a good American steak meal.

During these years, I spent countless hours away from the restaurant, which was not always ideal. If you have a restaurant, people want to see you and talk to you. Once, in the early years of our restaurant, I ran into one of our guests on the street and he complimented me on the wonderful dinner experience he and his wife had at Handke's Cuisine last week. I - not knowing any better - responded honestly saying, "I'm glad you enjoyed everything because I was unfortunately out of town for a couple of days." Then the gentleman added, "Well, my wife and I were thinking that it wasn't quite the same without you." From then on, when I was away and a guest asked if I could come to the table, the staff had strict orders to say, "The chef just had to step out for a moment to check on the catering." This worked.

Fundraisers also took us away from the restaurant. At some fundraisers we were the official caterer; for others we sponsored everything. One was for the Homeless Foundation. One of the board members approached me to donate 12 desserts for this event. The salads, appetizers and entrees were donated by a chain grocery store in town. When I asked who I would share the dessert table with, I found out that the lady had approached six or eight other restaurants with the same request. I told her we would participate under one condition: we would take care of the *entire* dessert table and get credit in the program. She agreed to it. On that evening, when I saw the guests arriving, I recognized a lot of them as our clientele from the restaurant.

When I saw what the grocery store was serving, I decided I did not want to associate with this event again unless I did *all* the food, and the board agreed. We went from 110 guests to over 250 in a matter of just five years.

The Homeless Foundation gala always took place in a private residence. One year Mr. and Mrs. Les Wexner opened their home for this event. At 250 guests, the board had to stop taking reservations. Everyone wanted to see the Wexner's house, and we had a crazy number of requests! For the Wexner dinner, we had to step up the quality of our food offerings. Meatballs and chicken wings were not on the menu. (We never did such things anyway.) For this special venue, we did terrines, pâtés, smoked salmon, smoked trout and salads - the finest of everything. While doing these big events, my greatest concern was always to use the best ingredients, serve most delectable meals, and make the guests happy. If our meal wasn't top notch, word of our shortcomings would have spread around very quickly and the restaurant would have suffered.

In the early 2000s, we started serving as the official caterer for some very large, off-premise events. We were paid for everything, and our price had to be right during the bidding process to qualify. One such large event was *Up on the Roof*, aptly named for its location atop the Ninth Avenue parking garage opposite The Ohio State University Wexner Medical Center. The cocktail reception took place on the sixth floor and dinner was served on the seventh/top floor in a large, air-conditioned tent. The proceeds from this event, with 900-1100 guests supported The James Cancer Hospital.

The first year we catered *Up on the Roof,* Ohio State contracted an events coordinator. We were responsible for the food service, and the events coordinator was in charge of the beverage service. I'm not sure what the coordinator was thinking because he only planned two bars for 1,000 guests. The lines were extremely long and people waited 45 minutes for a drink! To make matters worse, it was a beautiful, but hot September evening - 80 degrees at the cocktail hour with people sweating in their black-tie attire. We had plenty of unhappy guests that particular evening. The following year, Ohio State had a new event coordinator - Betty Garrett. There were 16 bars and the party ran like clockwork.

Logistics were the key to success at this event. We had to have the right number of service staff, the right number of chefs and the right menu. For the entrée, we always did a combination plate with beef donated by Michael's Finer Meats & Seafoods and a seafood item that we purchased. We had two work tents. One was the kitchen tent and the other was a break-down tent. Neither was very large, and we had to carefully plan our equipment placement. Another complication was that we had to transport everything by truck to the seventh floor of the garage by 6pm. Chilled items were left in the van with the air conditioning running full blast until the very last minute. The first year I borrowed hot boxes (where we stored the plated hot meals) from the Grand Hyatt Hotel. I delivered the hot boxes to the garage in the truck, but getting them up to the seventh floor was another story. We couldn't drive the truck in the garage because there wasn't enough vertical clearance. On top of that, the boxes were too large for the elevator. Pushing the boxes up seven floors didn't work because they were too heavy. In the end, I pulled them up two at a time with my new ML320 Mercedes-Benz. The event was later moved to the field house, where it was much easier to work.

Another really fun event was *Hat Day* at the Franklin Park Conservatory. It was a copycat of a similar luncheon in New York City, attended primarily by women, who dressed in their finest, including, of course, hats. You saw the most beautiful hat creations at this party. We started catering this party in 2001 for 210 attendees. Attendance grew every year and by the last year we did it (2008), we had 650 guests. Every year, the day before the event, I went to church and prayed that we would not have rain because it took place in a tent. In the beginning, they had a keynote speaker, like Carlton Varney, for example. Later, they had a style show with *Saks Fifth Avenue*, and they asked me to participate. I agreed on the condition that I would be the last person on the runway since I had to ensure that the food went out well first. I had a double star status: great chef and good-looking guy in a tuxedo with a bowler hat. I wanted to hang an umbrella from my arm as well, but they said they could not find one.

Whenever we catered large events, I insisted on a tasting with the event's responsible parties. I also photographed the food at this point, so my chefs would know how to plate the dish. The photo also served as "proof" of what the client originally agreed to. At one of these preliminary meetings, Mrs. Ann Wolfe and Mrs. Pam Farber were the event chairs. They indicated we should serve "chicken grapes." I prepared a grilled, free-range chicken breast and a delicious Marsala sauce with halved grapes in it. I served them their plates, and returned to the kitchen to bring out the next course. When I came back to their table, they looked kind of disappointed. They explained that they had expected diced chicken in a white sauce all rolled up in a French crepe. Chicken Crepes not Chicken Grapes. I guess I still sometimes have a language barrier.

Over the years, I really enjoyed catering. There were always challenges: heavy traffic on the way to the venue; wait staff that didn't show up; forgotten items; preparations that ran late. These obstacles kept it exciting. The catering business also complemented the restaurant with regard to advertising and marketing. After a successful catering event, we found that we picked up new customers at the restaurant.

When I drive through Columbus today, I see many venues where I catered. It's amazing to me how many parties we did - small parties here, large parties there, Christmas parties, birthdays, weddings, corporate events and more. We did it all.

During this time, the restaurant also thrived. Once in a while, we had a request for someone to rent the whole place. We did that a few times, but you can't do that too often or your regular customers get too upset.

We were also involved in catering some political fundraisers. One was for President Obama in 2007, shortly after he announced that he was running for President. One of our regular customers, Larry James, who was a partner in the law firm Crabbe, Brown & James next door, invited me to make hors d'oeuvres for a mid-day reception for 70 guests in the community room at The Miranova. Then, closer to the election in 2008, the GOP in Columbus organized an event for 250 guests for Senator John McCain in a private home in Dublin. We planned and cooked a nice hors d'oeuvres menu. Because Senator McCain was the official GOP candidate, he had FBI protection. We had to supply information for background checks for all of the employees who would work at the party. Everything was going smoothly until we arrived at the location with our catering van loaded with food. The FBI and their big, bomb-sniffing dogs searched the entire van! The FBI agents assured us that their dogs were not interested in the food, but I was a little nervous. Well, we made it through the inspection, but we were delayed for 20 minutes. Another funny thing about this event was the local GOP request. They explained that Senator McCain wouldn't have time to eat at the event since he had to converse with the guests. Therefore, they requested that we deliver 18 "Pigs in a Blanket" to his hotel room before the event. Definitely a first for us.

Once in a while, I even catered for myself. In 1993 when our oldest daughter Kirsten graduated from The Ohio State University College of Veterinary Medicine, Margot and I thought this was a wonderful time to take advantage of our catering business. On Friday, the day of graduation, we catered the official party for 800 people - students and their families - immediately following graduation in front of the College of Veterinary Medicine. It was nothing fancy. We served sodas and 6,000 finger sandwiches. We sliced cases and cases of cantaloupe, pineapple, honeydew melons and strawberries. Then on Sunday, we invited 35 people to our home for an afternoon brunch with wine and all the trimmings. We even had a harpist playing on our porch. Very classy. I said to Margot, "Let's do this again next year to celebrate Kirsten's one-year anniversary as a DVM and call it *Summer Fest*."

So in 1994, we had *Summer Fest* with a few friends. *Summer Fest* continued until 2005, getting larger each year. One year, our neighbors called the police because our guests had cars parked all over the place. To avoid this problem the following year, we invited the neighbors two houses down from us in every direction (we lived on a corner) to the party. No more complaints. That last year, 2005, we had 185 guests, and we decided to discontinue the party since it had outgrown our facilities. Our clients and friends were very disappointed about our decision.

Back at the restaurant, I had three young culinarians, who were the backbone of my culinary team. Justin, who we called Junior, was a graduate of the CIA and originally from Westerville. He did his externship with us and returned after graduation. He was always my assistant when I gave cooking classes. He loved to cook and was really into food. After his days off, he always came and told me all about what he had cooked. When he was ready to move on, he found a restaurant on Nantucket Island for the summer season and I made some connections for him at the Ritz Carlton in Naples for the winter season. He did this for several years. Then he moved to the Boston area and became *sous chef* at BRINE - a nice seafood restaurant. The company opened another restaurant and he became executive chef there. Justin made me really proud.

Another was Scott Pierce, who was originally from Toledo with a culinary education from Hocking College in Nelsonville, Ohio. In 2005, I coached a junior team from Hocking College, and they qualified as one of the four teams to compete at the national convention. Scott was the team captain and they came in third. I saw a lot of potential in Scott, and offered him a position at Handke's Cuisine after he graduated. I couldn't have made a better selection. Whatever you asked him to do, he did. He worked very precise and clean. He was always on time and never missed a day. He was one of the chefs who I could send to a catering job, and I didn't have to worry about anything. After we left the restaurant, he stayed on for a while. He worked at several restaurants in town and cooked for Mr. and Mrs. Wexner on a part-time basis. Eventually he got married and opened up a catering business in Toledo - Tree City Catering. He's doing very well.

Last but definitely not least there was Asa, who was originally from Cleveland and a CIA student, who was financing his education on his own. He started his externship with us in December 2003 - a very busy time of year. Sometimes we had to prepare for the next day after the restaurant closed in the evening - meaning we worked until 1 or 2am. After a week, I asked Asa whether he had rented a room somewhere in town and how he was settling in. He hadn't found a room yet, and he drove to Cleveland every night! That's what I call dedication! That's also when I knew that Asa really wanted to be a chef. I took him home with me a couple times when we worked late until he found his own place. During the four months of externship, he was an extremely hard worker, so I hired him after graduation. He became lead chef and eventually I promoted him to *sous chef*. When we sold the restaurant in 2008, he stayed on as executive chef until 2009, when the new owner closed Handke's Cuisine. A few months later, he found a new home at The Columbus Club on Broad Street, where management and members are very happy to have him. He serves excellent meals and runs a very clean kitchen. I have done several wine dinners with him at the club and whenever I needed assistance, he has helped me.

In 2006 we celebrated our 15th anniversary at Handke's Cuisine. We had done some great things and the restaurant was running well. We had a wonderful, supportive clientele and staff. We had done community fundraisers. But we were missing one thing: Margot and I could never take extended vacations. We saw each other every day, and enjoyed one meal together at the restaurant after the rush was over. Otherwise we didn't really have a private life. I left the house every morning, except Saturdays and Sundays, at 6:30, went shopping, and arrived at the restaurant by 8:45. Then, depending on the events of the day, I usually got home at 11pm or later. We talked about our problem and came to the conclusion that maybe it was time to sell and retire.

We had no idea, however, how to go about it. Through the recommendation of some friends, we found an appraiser to evaluate our business and a commercial real estate agent to find a buyer. Naturally, this had to be done very secretly. If our clientele learned that we were selling our restaurant, they might start seeking another venue where they could wine and dine. All meetings had to be either on Sundays when the restaurant was closed or at our home. We received a pretty good estimate of our assets; we signed a confidentiality contract; and the real estate agent found some interested parties. But everyone seemed to have the same problem - not enough money. They all had the great idea that we carry some of the debt, which was unacceptable to us. Things dragged on for quite some time until the real estate agent found someone who made an acceptable offer. We then drew up a contract and our last official day at the restaurant was Saturday, July 20, 2008.

Margot didn't come to the restaurant for the last couple of days because it was very hard for both of us to leave all of a sudden. The restaurant was like our second home and part of our family. But I had to be there to serve the last meal. Some of our regular clients came in to say goodbye and enjoy this final meal. I served many of our favorites that evening: *Fresh Morels in Madeira Cream Sauce with Angel Hair Pasta, Lobster Burgers with Sautéed Foie Gras on a Brioche Bun, Roasted*

Alaskan Halibut in Shiso Broth, *Chanterelle Mushroom And Corn Risotto*, *Dry Cured Roasted Duck Breast*, *Octopus Salad*, and *Sautéed Veal Steak with Colossal Maryland Crabmeat*.

It was sad that Margot was not with me during the last hours of Handke's Cuisine because she was as much a part of Handke's Cuisine as I was. But on the other hand, I understood why she didn't want to be there. We never would have been as successful as we were without her. I cannot thank her enough for all the years that we worked together in Germany and at Handke's Cuisine and throughout my entire career. She always stayed by my side and supported me. I didn't always make good decisions, and it was Margot who got us back on the right track. I don't think I could have achieved everything I did in my culinary career without her. We were - and are - a fantastic team.

Crème Brûlée
Yields 12 Portions

Ingredients

1 quart Heavy Cream (36% or 40%)
1 each Vanilla Bean, split in ½
8 each Large Egg Yolks
1 cup Granulated Sugar
1 cup Brown Sugar in the Raw (natural turbinado cane sugar)

Method

1. Preheat the oven to 325F.
2. Place the heavy cream and vanilla bean and seeds (scrape the seeds out of the bean with the back of a paring knife) in a sauce pot. Heat a little and let sit for 30 minutes.
3. Whisk the eggs with the granulated sugar.
4. Bring the cream to a simmer and than temper into the egg yolk - sugar mixture.
5. Strain everything through a chinois or fine mesh sieve into a bowl.
6. Using a 4oz ladle, portion the mixture into small oven-proof creme brûlée ramekins. In case you have bubbles on top of the custard mixture, burn them away with a torch.
7. Put the filled dishes in a sheet pan or preferably a deep baking dish. Add hot water to sheet pan or baking dish, ideally reaching halfway up the side of the ramekins.
8. Place the sheet pan or baking dish with the ramequins in the preheated oven and bake for 20 - 30 minutes until the custard is set.
9. Move the ramekins from the water bath to a dry sheet pan and let cool a little. Then move the ramekins into the refrigerator. Let chill for at least 4 hours before serving.
10. To finish the creme brûlée, sprinkle a thin layer of Sugar in the Raw on top of the custard and burn with a torch.
11. If desired, garnish with seasonal berries.

Shrimp Quesadilla
with Three Tomato Salsa
Yields 4 Portions

Ingredients

For the Shrimp Quesadilla:
1 oz Unsalted Butter
1 oz Shallots, fine diced
½ oz Garlic, fine diced
½ oz Jalapeno Pepper, seeded and fine diced
6½ oz Shrimpettes (400-500 count, salad shrimp)
2½ oz Flat Leaf Spinach, rough chopped
3¼ oz Pepper Jack Cheese, diced or grated
3¼ oz Sharp Cheddar Cheese
to taste Salt
to taste Freshly Ground Black Pepper
4 each 7" Flour Tortillas, toasted in a cast iron skillet and wrapped in foil to keep from drying
    out
4 each Fresh Cilantro Sprigs

For the Three Tomato Salsa:
4 oz Yellow Tomatoes, diced
4 oz Red Tomatoes, diced
4 oz Tomatillo, diced
1½ oz Red Onion, finely diced
2 Tbsp Rough Chopped Cilantro Leaves
½ oz Garlic, minced
½ oz Jalapeno, seeded and fine diced
1 oz Olive Oil
¾ oz Fresh Squeezed Lime Juice
to taste Salt
to taste Freshly Ground Black Pepper

Method

1. Sauté the shallots, garlic and jalapeno peppers in butter until translucent.
2. Add the shrimpettes and spinach, sauté until the spinach is wilted. Remove the skillet from the heat.
3. Add the cheese and fold it into the mixture. Season to taste with salt and black pepper.
4. Place an equal amount of filling across the center of each tortilla and roll the tortilla up. Cut the tortilla in half on a bias or as you wish.
5. Serve with the three tomato salsa and garnish with fresh cilantro sprigs.
6. Mix all of the ingredients together and let marinate for 2 hours.
7. Serve with the shrimp quesadillas.

Chilean Pisco Sour
Yields 1 Portion

Ingredients

4 each Ice Cubes
1 ½ Tbsp Confectionary Sugar
3 oz Chilean Pisco
1 oz Fresh Lemon or Lime Juice

Method

1. Place the ice cubes in a cocktail shaker, add the sugar, the Pisco and then the lemon or lime juice.
2. Shake vigorously until the sugar dissolves.
3. Taste and adjust the sweetness to your liking as necessary.
4. Strain and serve in a chilled cocktail glass.

Fresh Morels
in Madeira Cream over Angel Hair Pasta, Green Asparagus
Yields 6 Portions

Ingredients

For the morels:
3 Tbsp Unsalted Butter
2 Tbsp Fine Diced Shallots
1 lb Fresh Morels, cut in ½ or ¼ and washed
1/3 cup Madeira Wine
1½ cups Heavy Cream
to taste Salt
to taste Freshly Ground Black Pepper
2 Tbsp Short-cut Dill

For the angel hair pasta and green asparagus:
2 qt Water, seasoned with salt and boiling
8 oz Angel Hair Pasta
to taste Salt
to taste Freshly Ground Black Pepper
4 Tbsp Extra Virgin Olive Oil
1 Tbsp Chopped Parsley
18 pieces Green Asparagus
1 qt Boiling Salted Water
2 Tbsp Whole Unsalted Butter, room temperature
to taste Salt

Method

1. For the morels, in a large skillet, melt the butter and add the shallots; sauté until translucent.
2. Add the morels and sauté for another couple of minutes.
3. Add the Madeira and cook until the Madeira is almost evaporated.
4. Add the heavy cream and season with salt and pepper. Reduce the heavy cream by half, adjust the seasoning and the dill, remove from the heat, reserve and keep hot.
5. For the past and asparagus, cook the angel hair pasta al dente and strain.
6. Hold the strainer with the pasta under running hot water. Return to the pot, season with salt and pepper and add the olive oil and parsley.
7. At the same time cook the asparagus for 3 minutes and strain. Return to the pot, add the butter and season with salt.
8. Divide the angel hair pasta into 6 soup bowls, ladle an equal amount of morels on top of the pasta in each bowl.
9. Garnish each plate with pieces of asparagus. Serve immediately.

Lobster Burger
with Sautéed Foie Gras on Brioche Bun
Yields 6 Portions

Ingredients

Burger:
10 oz Raw Shrimp, 16/20 count, peeled and deveined
6 oz Unsalted Butter, room temperature
1 each Lemon, juiced
1 dash Tabasco
to taste Salt
to taste White Pepper
1 lb Lobster Meat, raw, small diced*
2 Tbsp Dill, short cut
1 oz Shallots, fine diced, sautéed in a little butter and chilled

Build:
12 each Brioche Buns, 1 ½" diameter
12 each Slices of Yellow Tomato, same diameter as buns
1 oz Yellow Frisée
2 oz Curried Potato Chips
2 oz Mache Greens, tossed with walnut oil vinaigrette
12 each Slices of Hudson valley Foie Gras, ¾ oz. each

Method

1. Place the shrimp in a food processor. Add the butter in three stages and purée. Add the lemon juice, Tabasco, salt and pepper.
2. Remove from the food processor and place in a bowl with the diced lobster meat. Add the dill and sautéed shallots. Mix all of the ingredients well and let rest in a refrigerator for two hours.
3. Shape the mixture into 12 equal patties and grill 2 minutes on each side. When the burgers are almost done, cook the foie gras in a heavy iron skillet to medium temperature.
4. Split the buns in half and toast both sides.
5. On the bottom half of each bun, place a slice of yellow tomato. Place the cooked lobster patty on top of the tomato. On top of the patty place a slice of sautéed foie gras. Put a little frisée on the foie gras. Cover with top of the bun.
6. Serve with curried potato chips and dressed mache greens immediately.

Note

Since raw lobster meat can be very difficult to remove from the shell, whole lobsters can be plunged into boiling water for a minute or two before taking the meat out. The lobster meat should be still kind of raw for this recipe.

Roasted Alaskan Halibut
(or Chilean Seabass) in Shiso Broth
Yields 4 Portions

Ingredients

For the Sable Fish:
4 each 4oz Halibut Filet, boneless and skinless
¾ cups Soy Sauce
3 Tbsp Sugar
2 Tbsp Mirin
2 Tbsp Sake
1 tsp Fresh Ginger, peeled and grated
1 tsp Fresh Garlic, grated
1 tsp Fresh Lemon Gras, fine chopped

For the Shiso Broth:
1 quart Cold. Chicken Stock
2 Tbsp Soy Sauce
2 tsp Mirin
2 tsp Rice Vinegar
1 tsp Grated Garlic
1 tsp Peeled and Grated Fresh Ginger
1 tsp Sugar
¾ lb Lean Ground Beef
2 each Egg Whites
to taste Salt
to taste Pepper

For the Garnish:
¾ oz Shiitake Mushrooms, cleaned, stemmed and thinly sliced; blanched
20 each Thin slices of Peeled Carrots, blanched
¾ cup Leeks, cut into ¼" squares, blanched
4 each Shiso Leaves, julienned

Roasted Alaskan Halibut
(or Chilean Seabass) in Shiso Broth

Methods

1. For the fish, prepare marinade. Place the halibut in the marinade for at least 3 hours.
2. At service time, remove the halibut from the marinade and dry with a paper towel.
3. Place the halibut filets on an oiled baking sheet and roast in a 425 degree F preheated oven until a deep mahogany brown color on the outside. Set aside and keep warm.
4. For the broth, place the first ten ingredients in a pot; mix well and bring to a simmer.
5. Simmer, same as for clarifying a consommé, for 30 minutes.
6. Strain through a coffee filter and set aside, keeping it hot.

To Serve

Divide the vegetables and broth into 4 bowls and place the roasted Alaskan halibut filet in the center of the bowl.

Chanterelle Mushroom and Corn Risotto
Yields 6 Portions

Ingredients

1 Tbsp Unsalted Butter
1 tsp Minced Garlic
1 Tbsp Minced Shallots
2 cups Small Chanterelles, quartered
3 cups Fresh Corn, cut from the cob
¼ cup White Wine
1½ cups Heavy Cream
to taste Salt
to taste Freshly Ground Black Pepper
¼ each Idaho Potato, peeled and finely grated (microplane)
2 Tbsp Grated Parmesan Cheese
2 Tbsp Short-cut (on the bias) Green Onions

Method

1. Sauté the shallots and garlic with in butter until translucent.
2. Add the chanterelles and cook for 2 minutes.
3. Add the corn and cook another 2 minutes.
4. Deglaze with white wine.
5. When the white wine is reduced to almost sec, add the heavy cream and season to taste with salt and pepper.
6. Bring everything to a boil, then grate the potato into the mixture and simmer for 2 minutes.
7. Add the Parmesan cheese and spoon the risotto into 6 bowls.
8. Sprinkle the short-cut green onions on top and serve immediately.

Dry Cured Roasted Duck Breast
Yields 6 Portions

Ingredients

1¾ oz Cardamom Seeds
¾ oz White Peppercorns
1 oz Garlic Powder
2 each Bay Leaves
¾ oz Coriander Seeds
½ oz Juniper Berries
1 ¾ oz Brown Sugar
1 ¼ oz Kosher Salt

Method

1. Combine all of the spices except for the brown sugar and kosher salt in a spice grinder (coffee grinder) and process to a coarse/fine powder. Remove from the grinder, put in a container and add the brown sugar and salt. Mix well.
2. Score the skin of the duck breast in a crosshatch fashion with squares not larger than 1/8". Rub the breast with the spice rub and allow to marinate for three hours.
3. Sear the duck breast in a hot skillet, skin side down first. Place on a roasting rack and cook at 375F to desired temperature.
4. You might have some spice rub left, which you can save for another time in a tightly sealed glass jar.

Octopus Salad
Yields 6 Portions

Ingredients

1 lb Octopus Tentacles, sliced ¼" thick while still warm
1 cup Small Diced Green Bell Peppers
1½ cups Seeded and Diced Roma Tomatoes
1 cup Small Diced Red Onions
¾ cup Olive Oil
2 Tbsp Sherry Wine Vinegar
to taste Sea Salt
to taste Freshly Ground Black Pepper
2 Tbsp Chopped Parsley

Method

1. Cook and drain the octopus.
2. Slice the octopus, while still warm, and add to the green bell pepper, tomatoes and onions. Mix well.
3. Add the olive oil, sherry wine vinegar, sea salt and freshly ground black pepper and chopped parsley. Mix well.
4. Chill for two hours before serving.

Sautéed Veal Steak

with Colossal Maryland Crabmeat, Whole Grain
Mustard Hollandaise, White Asparagus and Baby
Carrots

Yields 6 Portions

Ingredients

For the Veal:
3 ozx Unsalted Butter
6 each 5oz Veal Steaks, cut out from the veal loin
to taste Salt
to taste Freshly Ground Pepper
3 Tbsp All-purpose Flour
18 pieces Colossal Maryland crabmeat

For the Whole Grain Mustard Hollandaise:
3 each Egg yolks
3 Tbsp White Wine, dry
½ lb Unsalted Butter, melted and clarified at 100 degrees F
2 Tbsp Whole Grain Mustard
to taste Salt
to taste Freshly Ground Black Pepper

For the White Asparagus and Baby Carrots:
12 pieces Whole White Asparagus, well peeled
12 pieces Baby Carrots, peeled and cut in half lengthwise
2 oz Unsalted Butter
to taste Salt
to taste Freshly Ground Pepper

Sautéed Veal Steak

with Colossal Maryland Crabmeat, Whole Grain Mustard Hollandaise, White Asparagus and Baby Carrots

Methods

1. For the veal, put the butter in a skillet over medium heat until it turns slightly brown.
2. Season the veal steak with salt and pepper, dust in flour and put into the skillet.
3. Sauté the veal on both sides for approximately 2 ½ minutes until golden brown.
4. Remove the veal steak from the skillet and put on a warm platter and keep warm.
5. For the hollandaise place the egg yolks and white wine in a medium-sized stainless steel bowl.
6. Put two cups of water in a small pot that the bowl will fit on top off. Bring the water to a boil. Set the bowl on top of it. Using a piano wire whisk, beat the egg yolks and white wine to a soft peak and the color is a pale yellow.
7. Remove the bowl from the heat and whip in the clarified butter, little by little.
8. Add the whole grain mustard. Adjust the seasoning with salt and pepper.
9. For the asparagus and carruts, in two separate pots, cook the asparagus and carrots in lightly salted water until tender.
10. Take the vegetables out of the water and combine in a stainless steel bowl.
11. Add the butter and gently toss to coat the vegetables. Season with salt and pepper.

To Serve

Put a veal steak on the left side of the plate. Put 3 pieces of colossal crabmeat on each veal steak. Napé the crabmeat generously with the whole grain mustard hollandaise. Arrange 2 pieces of white asparagus and 4 carrots on the right side of the plate. Serve immediately.

Post-Restaurant Years

Can you imagine a chef who cannot eat for an entire week?

Monday, July 21 arrived. All of the sudden I no longer had a set schedule like getting up at 6:15am, making coffee, serving a cup to Margot at her bedside, leaving the house at 6:45am, going shopping at Meijer, arriving at the restaurant at 8:45am, unloading the van, putting away the food and so on. We still had chores, but the everyday routine was gone. However, we soon discovered that as a retired couple, we had less time than we did before.

To make a smooth transition of the sale, we offered the new owner of Handke's Cuisine any help he required. Asa, my *sous chef*, became the executive chef. Christian, our *maitre d'*, and most of the other staff stayed on as well. Although Margot even said that she could help him in the front, the new owner never took advantage of this. I still catered some of the larger events that I had previously booked for August, September and the holidays. Also, I felt it was my responsibility to do *HatDay* since I had started it. In 2009, it had increased to 675 guests, and I wanted to make sure it ran smoothly one last time. I also committed myself to the once-a-month cooking class until the end of the year. Even though I went to the restaurant several times each month, it felt strange to be there. In the restaurant that I had once managed, I was now viewed as an employee. With each passing month, the distance became more apparent.

In August 2008, I received an email from my friend Ed Janos, who was a culinary consultant for the Collier family (of Naples, Florida). The Colliers also owned a 22,500-acre ranch in Montana where they spent the summers. Ed informed me that the Colliers were in need of an executive chef for this Montana home, the Rocking C's Ranch. When I first received Ed's email, I put it aside. I didn't think I had time to take this position. After a while, however, I looked at the offer again and realized it was for 2009 (and not 2008). Now this was a different story! In 2009, I was wide open. So then I called Ed, and told him I wanted to learn more about the opportunity and to see the ranch. After Ed made all the arrangements, we flew to Bozeman, Montana at the beginning of October. The ranch was 130 miles northwest of Bozeman and the closest town was White Sulphur Springs - 30 miles southeast of the ranch. We rented a car in Bozeman, and it took us about two and a half hours to drive to the ranch.

We arrived on a beautiful fall day boasting gorgeous blue skies, puffy white clouds and pleasant temperatures. I had driven through Montana many years prior on a camping trip, but on this trip I was impressed by the size of the state. Although Montana is the fourth largest state in the nation, it has less than one million inhabitants. The road seemed to stretch straight out in front of us for miles. Even though the speed limit was 70 miles per hour, every so often, you could really test your car's power on these roads using pedal-to-the-metal driving style.

When I arrived at the ranch, Ed showed me around and introduced me to the ranch manager, Chad, and the officer manager, Becky. The beautiful, light wood kitchen was very well equipped with everything you can imagine. It reminded me of a kitchen in a really large home. It was not a commercial kitchen, but it was large enough to take care of 40-50 guests. Rocking C's Ranch is a completely private and gated working ranch. They have about 300 cattle and 30 horses on the property, and the famous trout-laden Smith River flows right through the grounds. I was impressed with the beautiful staff quarters. They offered Margot and me a log cabin with a kitchen, living room with fireplace, bedroom, bathroom and big front porch. There was even an adjoining garage for my Mercedes Benz ML500. I accepted the job, then inquired what Margot would do. When we agreed that she would run the dining room, we signed a 30-page contract.

Near the end of May we departed from Columbus for Montana. Ed was there to familiarize us with everything, and we started working the next day. Like I mentioned before, White Sulphur Springs is 30 miles southeast of the ranch. We called it White Sulphur Springs West and nicknamed our Greenbrier years White Sulphur Springs East. To get to White Sulphur Springs West from the ranch, we had to drive 15 miles on gravel roads and then 15 miles on paved roads. Upon our return to Columbus, my car desperately needed a total detailing job; it was just covered in dust.

We really enjoyed our time in Montana, but five months was a long time. By the middle of August, guests had tapered off, and we were only cooking for Mr. and Mrs. Collier. We found ourselves missing the big city. Helena and Bozeman are nice towns, but once in a while you just want to see a little more. During those five months in Montana, we drove 8,000 miles, exploring the state on our days off.

That summer, we enjoyed very good relationships with the 35 ranch employees. Mr. and Mrs. Collier, who were very nice people to work for, asked us to return the following year. We agreed, but to a shorter period of time - just two and a half months from June 1 to August 15. But sometimes, things go differently than planned.

At the beginning of May, during my yearly medical checkup, the doctors found something that they thought might be cancer. When I told them that we were going out of town for two and a half months, they recommended that I return for another examination at the end of June. I followed their orders. At the second exam, they determined that my cancer required surgery. When I told Mr. and Mrs. Collier about my problem, they released me from my contract.

We left Rocking C's Ranch on July 16 and arrived in Columbus the very next day. I met with my surgeon on July 20, and had esophageal surgery on July 22. I had to stay in the hospital for seven days with nothing to eat or drink. Other than a little lollipop to wet my lips, all of my nourishment was intravenous. Can you imagine a chef who cannot eat for an entire week? Horrible. Just horrible. When I returned home, I unfortunately wasn't allowed to drive for three weeks. Of course, Margot was an excellent chauffeur. Since the surgery, I have had a medical checkup every six months. So far, so good.

In September 2010, we traveled to Europe with some friends on a celebration tour. Margot and I had big birthdays as well as a semi-big wedding anniversary. On this trip, we visited Baden-Baden, Munich, Salzburg and Sterzing (in Tyrol), and had a great time. Everyone enjoyed it.

Another thing we have become accustomed to is taking cruises. In 1981, we took a cruise with some friends from Miami to the Caribbean. After seven days, I could hardly wait to get off the darn boat. We didn't cruise again until 2005, when we went to Alaska. However, I really enjoyed that cruise. Since then, we've cruised the Mediterranean, the Far East, South America, Polynesia, Australia and New Zealand. I loved them all. In fact our next one - Sydney to Singapore - is already booked!

Margot is not always too happy that we are on the road so often. But I remind her that we have to do it as long as we can, as long as we have our health. She even mentioned a few times that instead of buying a new house, which we did in 2010, we should have bought a hotel room; it would've been much cheaper. I thought buying a house was necessary because I needed a bigger kitchen with a better stove. Naturally Margot wanted to downsize, but the problem was: bigger kitchens come with bigger houses.

Although we have very few relatives left in Germany, Margot still has some very close friends in Baden-Baden and I have some former work colleagues, who we like to visit every year. So we go to Baden-Baden every year, make small tours into the Black Forest and also do some hiking. Once in a while, we take a dinner trip to the Alsace-Lorraine region with their small restaurants that serve foie gras and frog legs. It's a nice change.

I've also been to Shanghai and Beijing twice in my retirement. Our neighbor at the Montana ranch, Mr. Hung Gu, a Chinese language and culture professor from Shanghai at Eckerd College in St. Petersburg, Florida, mentioned to me one evening that he was taking a group of business students on a three-week trip to Shanghai and Beijing. I asked him right away if he wanted another fare-paying student. He said, "Why not." He'd let me know when they'd be leaving. Since this conversation took place in June and a lot of other things happened the following months, I more or less forgot all about it. However, three days after we returned from Europe in October 2010, I received an email from the professor saying they were leaving January 4. "If you want to come along, get your own ticket and join us in Detroit." Two days later, I was all set to go. On January 4, I was with the professor and his group on my way to Shanghai. We stayed overnight near the airport in Shanghai, and the next morning we took the high-speed train to Beijing. Incredible. The train sped along at over 300 kilometers per hour and boasted a very smooth ride. And all of the things that I saw and experienced were fantastic: I climbed part of the Great Wall; I saw the Forbidden City; and I saw the Ming Tombs, where they buried the emperors. After three days in Beijing, we traveled back to Shanghai, where the students made interesting presentations to big companies on all kinds of business topics. On the weekend the professor introduced me to his family and friends. I was invited to their homes as well as to restaurants, where I watched their food preparation and enjoyed all kinds of meals.

I also celebrated the Chinese New Year with everyone. The fireworks all over Shanghai were unbelievable - they were everywhere, going up one after the next! It started at four in the afternoon and lasted until daybreak the next morning. In Shanghai, I went up the Oriental Pearl Tower, visited the Urban Planning Exhibition Center, and took in the popular tourist sites in the city. During these three weeks, I was absolutely overwhelmed that I had the opportunity to experience all of this at my age. Upon my return to Columbus, I told Margot about what I had seen, and promised to take her to China.

In March 2014, the Dublin Chamber of Commerce offered a nine-day trip to China. It was reasonable, so we booked it right away. We took a bus to Kennedy International Airport in New York City, since it was March when the weather is unpredictable. We did not by any means want to miss our flight to Beijing... you cannot walk there! Our tour consisted of 29 people on a full-sized bus. It was an excellent tour - very well organized with a talented English-speaking tour guide. We stayed at very good hotels, and had a great time. In Shanghai, we met with

Professor Hung's sister, Jenny, who spent the whole day giving us a really neat sight-seeing tour of Shanghai. When she and her husband visited us in Columbus in 2012, we took them to *Picnic with the Pops* one evening. We still remain in contact, emailing every so often.

Two years ago Margot and I celebrated our 50th wedding anniversary. So we invited the whole family - Kirsten and husband, Mike, Susi and her husband, Nick, and their children Johanna and Theo - to celebrate with us in Germany. We all arrived in Frankfurt, Germany at the beginning of May, and we picked up two rental cars - we couldn't all fit in one. Our first stop was my hometown, Schotten, where we stayed for three days. Kirsten and Susi were familiar with the town, but their husbands were not. We had our first celebration dinner at the same hotel, where we had celebrated our wedding 50 years ago. Naturally, since I didn't want to take any chances, I had planned the menu ahead of time. From there we went to Baden-Baden, Margot's hometown, for another celebration with friends. After three days in Baden-Baden, we drove to Dresden for another celebration there since I was born in Kamenz, a small town nearby. We spent a delightful two weeks with everyone. When our family flew home, we stayed on to enjoy the anniversary gift they had given us - a five-day trip to Berlin.

Instead of going by car, the girls purchased first-class train tickets for us with reserved seats on the ICE high-speed train. It only took five hours to travel from Baden-Baden to Berlin. For long-distance travel, this is definitely the way to go - it's very relaxing. It was such a memorable trip. Berlin is such a vibrant city! We toured the Reichstag, took city tours with the *Hop-on, Hop-off Bus*, saw the Brandenburg Gate, the Berlin Wall Memorial and the famous Checkpoint Charlie, had dinner at the TV tower and cruised the Havel River, which runs right through the city.

We recently traveled to Australia and New Zealand, where we visited the Queen Victoria Market in Melbourne and the Fish Market in Sydney. We even saw the vicious Tasmanian devil in Tasmania. We also spent two weeks in Portland, Oregon, where I cooked a dinner for 25 people hosted by Susi's boss, Mr. Ernie Spada.

My life has turned out exactly as I planned it: I am a chef and I have seen so much of the world! I'm excited for our next adventure. *Food is Fun: Let's cook and eat!*

Afterword

A lot people in Columbus ask me which local restaurants I recommend. I always try to avoid this question and tell them not to ask me questions like that. If they insist, I give them our home address. Margot and I love to entertain! It's such fun to watch our guests eat - to see their faces when they take a bite of something that they find particularly pleasant. I also take note of what they don't finish eating, so I can continue to shape my recipes to cater to their every-changing tastes.

What I find fascinating is the role wine plays in enhancing food flavors. The body, flavor and aroma of wine dramatically change the dining experience. It is absolutely critical to the meal's success to select appropriate wines. If I want to be really sure that the wine pairs perfectly with the dish I am preparing, I consult a sommelier. I am lucky to have a great friend, Greg Maurer of Heidelberg Distributing, who is a long-term executive in the wine industry. When he comes to dinner, I share the menu with him in advance. Then, he selects the wine!

Here is a menu that I recently prepared for a small group of friends. The wines that are listed with each dish were closely paired by Greg to complement the food. Would you like to come to dinner?

HORS D'OEUVRES

House Smoked Salmon and Dill Cream Cheese Pinwheels on Rye Bread

Steak Tartare with French Bread

Sautéed Black Tiger Shrimp with Lime, Sweet Chili Sauce & Cilantro Glacé

Country Paté on Melba Toast with Lingonberry Relish
G.H. Mumm Champagne Brut 'Cordon Rouge' Non Vintage

MENU

Porcini Cappuccino
En Route Russian River Valley 'Les Pommiers' Pinot Noir 2013

Sous Vide Alaskan Sablefish with Lobster and Scallop Mousseline with Poached White
Asparagus, Sauce Hollandaise
Far Niente Napa Valley Chardonnay 2014

Pink Texas Grapefruit Sorbet with Campari and Rosemary

Sautéed Hudson Valley Foie Gras on Toasted Brioche, Poached Granny Smith Apple Julienne,
Frisée with Hazelnut Oil
Château Doisy Daene Barsac Grand Vin de Sauternes 2009

Kagoshima Japanese Black A-5 Wagyu Steak, Black Truffle Fritters, Vegetable Fricassee
Opus One Napa Valley Red Wine 2012

Spring Greens, Greenbrier Chèvre Soufflé
Honig Napa Valley, Rutherford Sauvignon Blanc 'Reserve' 2014

Seasonal Fruit and Berries with a Riesling Sabayon and Red Wine Granité
Dr. Loosen 'Urziger Wurzgarten' Riesling Auslese 2013

Recipe Index